COMING SHORTLY:
"NOW WE'RE IN THE AIR"

WALLACE BEERY and RAYMOND HATTON.

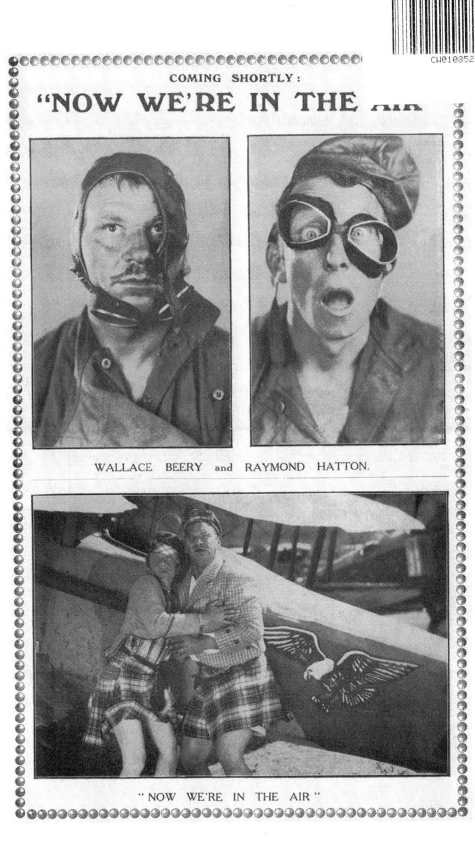

" NOW WE'RE IN THE AIR "

Now We're in the Air

Now We're in the Air
(A Companion to the Once "Lost" Film)

with a foreword by Robert Byrne

Thomas Gladysz

Cover design by Christy Pascoe

A publication of the Louise Brooks Society

www.pandorasbox.com

All images from the collection of
Thomas Gladysz / Louise Brooks Society
unless otherwise indicated

Copyright © 2017 Thomas Gladysz

All rights reserved, including the right of
reproduction in whole or in part in any form

ISBN-13: 978-0692976685

ISBN: 069297668X

DEDICATION

To Robert Byrne, thanks to you
another silent film will once again
see the light of day, or rather,
the darkness of a theater.

To the pole sitters of the 1920s,
those silly kids up in the air to whom
the film was originally dedicated.

And to Christy Pascoe, companion in my work,
I know I should be working on something else....
but the idea for this book just flew into my head.

SKY scrappers, these two—zooming
down to a laugh landing. Nose dives
and parachute leaps guaranteed to make
any self-respecting aviator green with
envy.

CONTENTS

Acknowledgments 11

Foreword 13
by Robert Byrne

1 The Film 17

2 The Press Sheet Story 27

3 *Boy's Cinema Weekly* 33

photo supplement - 43
the restored fragment

4 *La Novela Paramount* 51

5 "The Air Recruits" 83

photo supplement - 99
publicity images

6 In Czechoslovakia 105

7 Lulu's Black Tutu 109

8 Film Credits & Trivia 113

9 Further Reading 121

About the Author 127

ACKNOWLEDGMENTS

My
sincere gratitude to Kevin Brownlow,
Robert Byrne, Barry Paris, Christy Pascoe,
and
Ira
Resnick, each of whom directly or indirectly contributed to this project. Thanks
also to Pamela Hutchinson, the gracious Lynne Watson & Ryan Campbell, Jay
Weissberg, and Enrique Zulberti. I also wish to acknowledge the following
institutions and websites for their varied assistance: Le Giornate del Cinema Muto;
Internet Movie Database; National Library of the Czech Republic; Louise Brooks
Society; Margaret Herrick Library, Academy of Motion Picture Arts and
Sciences;
Media
History
Digital
Library;
Národní
filmový
archive;
Newspapers.com;
San Francisco Public Library;
San Francisco Silent Film Festival.

*Images courtesy of
Robert Byrne /
San Francisco
Silent Film Festival*

12

FOREWORD

BY ROBERT BYRNE

There is magic in the movies.

With a grand sweep of his arm, top-hatted Monsieur Chelaine gestures elaborately to the nearby circus caravan. Open swings the wagon door and out steps the living, breathing, *and moving* incarnation of still photograph I have seen a thousand times before. It is Louise Brooks as Grisette making her entrance in Frank Strayer's *Now We're in the Air*. Dressed in her fetching black tutu my eyes are riveted on the 21 year-old Brooks as she descends the stairs behind the wagon. If there are other actors present in the frame they might as well be on the moon.

If you search the internet for images of Louise Brooks the first photos that you likely encounter are portraits of the actress posing in the black tutu. For decades, film stills and Eugene Robert Richee's studio portraits of Lulu in her tutu were how we came to know *Now We're in the Air*. These still images were all we had, tantalizing snapshots representing a film that had not been seen for generations and for which not a single frame of motion picture film was known to survive.

In October 2016, I paid a visit to the Národní filmový archiv, the national film archive of the Czech Republic, on behalf of the National Film Preservation Foundation. I was there to assess unique nitrate copies of selected American silent films in their collection. In addition to my targeted list I also brought along own personal wish-list of titles, and for this visit to Prague I supplemented my agenda with a set of recommendations from Kevin Brownlow who clearly had some ideas of what I might be able to see.

There followed a glorious week at the archive graciously hosted by director Michal Bregant, head curator Briana Čechová, and curator Veroslav Haba. I reveled in the wealth of their collection and benefited from the dedication, professionalism, and especially the hospitality, of the entire archive staff.

Exceeding all hopes, I was astonished to learn that the archive held nitrate material for *Now We're in the Air*. What they had was not complete, the cans held 552 meters out of the original 1,767, but I knew immediately that we would be undertaking a project to restore what remained. The film was originally released in six reels and the surviving material included sections of the second, third, and final reel. The good news was that even though we were dealing with fragments each of the three sections presented representative and cohesive segments of the film, and of course we had the wonderful bonus of Grisette's introduction and entrance.

Even though we were dealing with just a twenty-two minute fragment, the project to restore the film required almost every trick in the book. Our raw material was the 552 meters of 35mm nitrate film, tinted orange, with Czech language intertitles, and some sections exhibiting a moderate level of chemical decomposition. The goal of our restoration was to put the three fragments back in their original sequence, replace the Czech intertitles with original American release intertitles, restore the image to the extent reasonably possible and within the bounds of ethical guidelines, and to produce a new 35mm preservation negative and tinted 35mm film prints.

The final result was a great success that was only possible through an incredible international team effort. It begins and ends with Národní filmový archive who has safeguarded the film for all these years and who generously made it available. It was also NFA that supervised the color-dye tinting of the new 35mm prints, so they were genuinely the first and last stop on our journey. In between those two points were Thomas Gladysz and Christy Pascoe of the Louise Brooks Society who carried out crucial research on the film, including transcription of the original film continuity from which we were able to re-create the American intertitles. The film grading and 35mm negative were produced at Haghefilm in Amsterdam, Netherlands and the 35mm black and white film prints struck at the Library of Congress Packard Campus for Audio Visual Conservation in Culpeper, Virginia. These prints then traveled back to Prague where the original amber dye-tinting was applied by Jan Ledecky and Karel Wagner. Last but certainly not least was San Francisco Silent Film Festival board member Ira Resnick, who provided vital underwriting and without whom the project to restore *Now We're in the Air* would not have been possible.

Looking back, I am still astonished by the amount of attention that has been lavished up our little twenty-two minute fragment. Even with what remains we have far too much Berry and Hatton and far too little Brooksie, but what we do have is magic, and isn't that what this book is all about?

¶ The screen's first comedy team (in time and quality) has re-enlisted! They've quit fighting foney fires and they're again fighting (?) for Uncle Sam. Daffy doughboys in "Behind the Front", goofy gobs in "We're in the Navy Now," they're loony Lindberghs in "Now We're in the Air." — And how! ¶ You expect us to say "best Beery-Hatton yet". Well, we don't have to. See the picture; then *you'll* say it for us! The human being isn't born yet who can watch without splitting his medulla oblongata with laughter these boys taking the air in bronco-busting balloons, bilious biplanes and parachutes that even aces can't open. ¶ Luscious Louise Brooks twice the eyeful she usually is because she plays twin sisters. Frank Strayer production. Get all set for another Paramount record-menacer, gentlemen. And how thick and fast these Big Ones have been coming from Paramount this fall!

THE FILM

Had it not been for its rediscovery in 2016, *Now We're in the Air* may well have remained a lost *and* a forgotten movie. Today, most all agree it is an enjoyable, though rather silly and largely inconsequential film. It has its moments. What redeems it in our 21st century eyes is the presence of Louise Brooks. Though she has little to do, her appearance gives this otherwise stumbling slapstick comedy a bit of spark.

Brooks' brief tenure in Hollywood began in 1927, the year *Now We're in the Air* was made. With her stardom on the rise, she transitioned from Paramount's East Coast operations (where she had started in films in 1925) to the West Coast and Hollywood. Considered an up-and-coming actress, Brooks was cast in important parts in four major releases. Until recently, each of those four films was considered lost, denying contemporary viewers a chance to see the actress at the near peak of her American career.

Brooks' first Hollywood film was *Evening Clothes*, a sophisticated romantic drama in which the young actress plays a woman of low repute opposite leading man Adolphe Menjou. It was followed by *Rolled Stockings*, a breezy tale of romance and rivalry set on a college campus; aimed at the youth market, the film featured the Paramount Junior Stars, and proved popular. Next came two movies made and released back-to-back: *The City Gone Wild*, a big city crime drama directed by James Cruze in which Brooks plays a moll, and the Wallace Beery – Raymond Hatton comedy *Now We're in the Air*. The latter film was the last to go into production, though the third released.

Described as an aviation burlesque, *Now We're in the Air* concerns a pair of "aeronuts" (also called "looney Lindberghs" and "batty balloonitics") who wander near the front lines during wartime. Along the way, they meet twins named Grisette and Griselle. Brooks plays the twins, one raised French, one raised German, who become the romantic interest of the two would-be heroes. Hatton falls for the French twin, and Beery for the German. Despite their affections, the two can't tell the twins apart, and some of the film's humor springs from repeated instances of mistaken identity. Unfortunately, the surviving footage only includes Brooks in the role of the French twin, Grisette, a carnival worker dressed in a dark tutu marked with her initial, "G." The noted French actor and director Émile Chautard plays Brooks' father, the carnival owner.

Moving Picture World summarized the film's thin plot this way: "Wally and Ray are cousins intent upon getting the fortune of their Scotch grand-dad, an aviation nut. They become mixed-up with the U. S. flying corps and are wafted over the enemy lines in a runaway balloon. Through misunderstanding they are honored as heroes of the enemy forces, and sent back to the U. S. lines to spy. Here they are captured and almost shot, but everything ends happily."

In the 1920s, Beery and Hatton were teamed in a number of popular *Dumb and Dumber*-like comedies. With its aviation-theme, *Now We're in the Air* was the third of the mismatched pair's farcical "service comedies," following the army-themed *Behind the Front* (1926) and the naval-themed *We're in the Navy Now* (1926).* Notably, Brooks' then-husband, Eddie Sutherland, directed the two earlier comedies, each of which did good box office and were deemed worthy of a successor.

Now We're in the Air was shot between August 1 and September 8 at the Paramount studio near Hollywood, as well as at the Lasky Ranch, a local aviation field, and at an amusement pier in nearby Venice. There was, as well, aerial footage shot in the area, though most of the action shown in both the balloon and airplane scenes was shot in front of a filmed backdrop. Also made use of in the film's final scene was the then recently built faux ocean liner on the corner of the Paramount lot, back of Marathon street and a block north of Melrose.

The film's working title was first reported as *Taking the Air*, and then *We're in the Air Now*. At the end of December, 1926, the *Hollywood Citizen News* reported Budd Schulberg had assigned famed comedian Larry Semon to write the story. However, nothing seems to have come of it. An outline by Tom J. Geraghty and a treatment by John F. Goodrich was completed by February 3, 1927. Later drafts reworked various

---

* Brooks' first "appearance of-a-kind" in the Beery–Hatton service comedies was in *We're in the Navy Now* (1926). Brooks and director Eddie Sutherland were newly married when Sutherland cut short their honeymoon to return to Hollywood to begin work on the naval comedy. In a nod to his absent bride (then still working on the East Coast), Sutherland named the ship seen in the film the "U.S.S. Louise."

elements, including the title. Among the actors who were first considered for the film but did not appear in it were Ford Sterling, Zasu Pitts, Spec O'Donnell, and Tom Kennedy. The latter had appeared in the two prior Beery-Hatton service comedies.

Early on, renown Swedish director Mauritz Stiller, *The City Gone Wild* director James Cruze, and even *Wings* director William Wellman were each announced as piloting the project. Paramount staff director Frank R. Strayer, then at the height of his largely undistinguished career, was eventually assigned the task. Brooks told Kevin Brownlow that Strayer was passive in his direction, letting the cameramen and actors take over the action in a scene.

Harry Perry, who had an exceptional command of aerial photography, served as the film's cinematographer. Perry worked on two other significant aviation pictures, *Wings*, from earlier in 1927, and *Hell's Angels* (1930), for which he was nominated for an Academy Award. Interestingly, a notation in the script for *Now We're in the Air* called for the use of unused footage from the Wellman-directed and Perry-filmed *Wings*, another war movie and the first film to win an Academy Award for Best Picture. Aerial footage shot for *Wings*, in fact, can be seen in *Now We're in the Air*, near the end of the surviving footage. It stands out.

Despite the use of footage from an earlier Paramount production, the studio put fresh money and resources into *Now We're in the Air*. Notably, six wind machines were used during the making of the film, which led to a risky stunt reported in the *New York Times* where Beery and Hatton wander onto a field as a flight squadron is taking off. The gust of the combined motors (the six wind machines and a dozen airplane propellers) tore-off their Scottish Highlander garb and lifted the duo off the ground and out of the view of the camera.

Fifteen airplanes, including a Spad, scout planes, and a couple of American, twin-motored Martin Bombers (one of which was disguised as a German Gotha), were used during the making of the film. One Martin Bomber was flown to the production by Marine Corps Captain Harold Campbell, who served as a technical advisor. In one of the film's "big thrill scenes" (near the end of the surviving footage), a 76-foot Martin Bomber was deliberately wrecked in a spectacular battlefield crash.

One special effect Paramount wasn't ready to employ was sound, which was then just coming in. According to the Barry Paris biography, Brooks once suggested there was some thought given to adding dialogue to the film. However, the distinction of the first Paramount film to include spoken dialogue went to the subsequent Brooks-Beery film, *Beggars of Life* (1928).

Now We're in the Air was widely and generally favorably reviewed. However, some critics thought its humor rather worn. *Motion Picture* opined, " . . . you have a picture fairly creaking and groaning with the struggle to be funny and sadly lacking in the true comedy spirit." The *New York Post* wrote "Mr. Beery and Mr. Hatton have been seen so often to kick each other that it has ceased exactly to be the fountain of wit." Mourdant Hall of the *New York Times* thought it "no better and probably no worse than the other pseudo-comic exploits of this pair."

A few critics commented on the film's crude humor, especially the scene where Wally and Ray's kilts are blown away and reveal more than was thought seemly, while others reacted negatively to the scene involving a cow (which in the scenario was described as dead). The *New York American* thought the film "often vulgar." *TIME* magazine thought it "descended into extraordinarily vulgar farce." Exhibitors were also taken aback. The manager of the Paramount theatre in Wyoming, Illinois thought there was "Quite a bit of smut" in the movie. Similarly, the manager of the Strand theatre in Paoli, Indiana noted, "The sequence with a prop cow is decidedly vulgar. When the sub-title 'You can't make a cow's hind-end out of me,' appeared on the screen, the few ladies in the audience beat a hasty retreat." In Kansas, the film was only approved for exhibition by the state's Board of Review "with eliminations."

Though some winced at its crude humor (not evident in the surviving material), the Beery-Hatton film proved to be one of the more popular comedies of 1927. It is, arguably, the most popular of any of Brooks' American silents.

Generally liked by local critics, the film did good box office where ever it showed. In New York City, it enjoyed an extended run, as it did in San Francisco, where it proved to be one of the biggest hits of the year. At a time when most new releases played only one week, *Now We're in the Air* ran for more than a month in the City by the Bay, where it was extended three times due to robust ticket sales. In Boston, it also did well, opening simultaneously in five theaters in the area. The *Boston Evening Transcript* noted, "… most of the audience at the Washington Street Olympia this week were so moved by mirth that they were close to tears. Presumably the experience has been the same at the Scollay Square Olympia, the Fenway, the Capitol in Allston and the Central Square in Cambridge." Newspapers in other cities like Atlanta, Georgia and St. Louis, Missouri reported a similar reception.

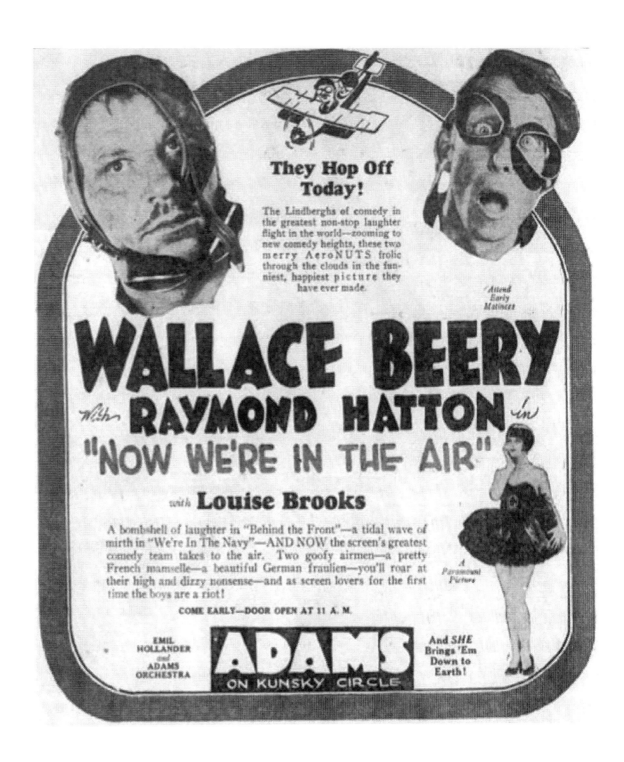

As advertised in Detroit, Michigan in December, 1927. The film was popular in the auto town, enough so to be extended an extra week. It returned for a short run the following month.

Looking past Beery and Hatton's antics, critics took notice of Brooks, who played the twins. The *New Orleans Item* stated, "The added feature of *Now We're in the Air* is the presence of Louise Brooks as the heroine. One of the cleverest of the new stars, she has immense ability to appear 'dumb' but like those early Nineteenth Century actresses, commended by Chas. Lamb, she makes the spectators realize that she is only playing at being dumb."

Some thought Brooks had little to do in the film besides show off her well regarded legs, but for others, her dual role made the film. The *San Francisco News* stated, "Both the hulking and ungainly Beery and the cocky little Hatton give goofingly good accounts of themselves. Then there is Louise Brooks. She's the girl—or the girls—in the case, for Louise is twins in the story, and about this fact much of the comedy is woven." Across town, the *San Francisco Bulletin* added, "Louise Brooks is the leading woman of this picture. She appears as the twin sisters. This results in some remarkable and very interesting double exposures."

The New York *Morning Telegraph* wrote, "Louise Brooks is seen as the feminine lead. She essays the role of twins. Which, if you know Louise, is mighty satisfactory. She is decorative enough to admire once, but when you are allowed the privilege of seeing her double, the effect is devastating." The *Boston Post* added, "You see there are pretty twin sisters, Grisette and Griselle, both played by the fetching Louise Brooks, who marry Wally and Ray, who cannot tell their wives apart except by their dogs, one a poodle, one a dachshund."

Throughout 1928 and 1929 and into 1930, *Now We're in the Air* was shown all around the world—in Latin America, throughout Europe (including the then Czechoslovakia), and in countries in Africa and Asia. And though it was a silent film, *Now We're in the Air* continued to be shown well into the early sound era in the United States. Advertisements promoting it pop-up in newspapers in smaller American towns not yet wired for sound as late as 1929, and even in Fairbanks, Alaska (pre-statehood) in early 1930. In December, 1931 it was screened in the city of Darwin in the Northern Territory, Australia.

After that, the film seems to have faded into obscurity. *Now We're in the Air* was seldom remembered let alone mentioned except in connection with Wallace Beery as a way to explain the actor's well known love of flying—he reportedly first flew while the making of the film. *Now We're in the Air* was also referenced a few times in late 1937 and early 1938 when American newspapers ran "10 Years Ago Today" columns recalling the films then playing locally. In 1941, Paramount revaluated its story property while searching for material for new films. The evaluation comment read: "This is material suitable only for a short comedy and might be sold for this purpose."

Though largely forgotten in the years that followed, *Now We're in the Air* would play a small though pivotal part in Brooks' later life. In the 1998 documentary, *Louise Brooks: Looking for Lulu*, renowned film publicist John Springer recalled how, around 1946, he came to meet Brooks, then living a down-and-out existence. Unknown to Springer, the actress happened to live across the hall in their modest New York City apartment building.

"After I got out of the Air Force I came to New York. There was a woman across the hall. As soon as she would see anybody she would put her hand up like this and put her bag covering her face. I thought she was kind of nutsy. Then one night we had a party. We decided to make it a silent movie party. And we made posters. Put them up in the entrance to the apartment house, in the hall way. 'This way to see Louise Brooks in the air.' And in the middle of the party suddenly there was a furious knock at the door. I opened the door. It was Miss Brooks from across the hall. 'How dare you make fun of me like that? How dare you?' Suddenly it hit me. God. That's Louise Brooks."

A few years later, in 1953, Springer was talking with James Card, film curator at the George Eastman House in Rochester, New York. According to Springer, Card remarked, "I would give anything to talk to Louise Brooks. Nobody knows where she is or what's happened to her. I don't suppose you would even know." Springer's hallway encounter, which is also recalled in the Barry Paris biography, would lead to a lasting if fragile friendship between the young film publicist and the long off-the-screen actress, then in her early forties. Springer replied, "I know her very well."

A party invitation evoking the long forgotten *Now We're in the Air* was the first link in a chain of events that would lead Brooks to relocate to Rochester, where she reacquainted herself with her earlier career, blossomed as a writer, authored *Lulu in Hollywood*, and experienced something rare in American culture—a second life.

As advertised in Indianapolis, Indiana—October 1927

WALLACE RAYMOND

BEERY AND HATTON

IN

NOW WE'RE IN THE AIR

LOUISE BROOKS

a *Paramount Picture*

Special 3' x 10' Colored Banner

Comical Aeronuts Run Riot in the Clouds!

Film Facts

The Stars

WALLACE BEERY and Raymond Hatton are the greatest stars comedy has ever produced. The box office and the public clamor for their wares verifies this. One after another, their pictures achieve new records. Louder and louder grow the laughs at their inimitable antics. And now they've topped everything they ever did.

The Supporting Cast

Louise Brooks as the leading lady was one of the happiest selections ever made in Hollywood. Young, beautiful, charming, and in this picture she's doubly so, because she's twins. In other words, she has a dual role. She is French and German as well as clever and cunning in this picture. You'll remember Louise in "Rolled Stockings," "Evening Clothes," "It's the Old Army Game," and "The American Venus."

Malcolm Waite is the roughest ruffian, and the heaviest heavy, cinematically speaking, in Hollywood. His villainy will make a chill run down your back and when the laugh is on him it's just twice as enjoyable. He's been in the Beery-Hatton pictures before. Remember him as the German spy in "We're in the Navy Now"?

The rest of the cast is composed of the most capable players available in the Hollywood free-lance field. Emile Chautard, veteran character actor, who played Adolphe Menjou's father-in-law in "Blonde or Brunette," is the girl's father in this. Duke Martin who played the gangster in Thomas Meighan's picture, "The City Gone Wild," is the hard-boiled top sergeant; Russell Simpson, famous character actor, is Lord Abercrombie McTavish and all others in the cast are of equal distinction and merit.

Authors

Monte Brice and Keene Thompson. Monte Brice was responsible in part for the former Beery-Hatton successes, "Behind the Front," "We're in the Navy Now." He directed Wallace Beery in "Casey at the Bat." Keene Thompson, assisted Brice in writing "Now We're in the Air."

Scenarist

Tom J. Geraghty who has written the scenarios for some of the last few years' biggest hits. He wrote the scenario for "Now We're in the Air."

Type of Picture

A laugh riot. Beery and Hatton, as two ship stokers who are made ill even by a roller-coaster, suddenly find themselves blown into the air service during war time.

Locale

France and Germany.

Cast

Wally	Wallace Beery
Ray	Raymond Hatton
Griselle Chelaine,	
Grisette Chelaine,	
	Louise Brooks
Lord Abercrombie McTavish	Russell Simpson
Monsieur Chelaine	
	Emile Chautard
Professor Saenger,	
	Malcolm Waite
Top Sergeant	Duke Martin

WALLACE BEERY RAYMOND HATTON *IN* NOW WERE IN THE AIR *with* LOUISE BROOKS *a Paramount Picture*

Gloom takes a nose dive!

THEY were soldiers and sailors — now they are goofy airmen.
High-flyers in comedy, this pair!

Two-column Supplementary Press Ad 2AS

The Story

WALLACE BEERY and Raymond Hatton are a couple of ship stokers who have been engaged as servants by Russell Simpson, who is a gouty old Scotchman, Lord Abercrombie McTavish. Simpson wants to enlist in the air service during the last year of the war. He visits a Flying Circus to see how altitude agrees with him. This makes him sure he can fly a plane; but Beery and Hatton are terrified from start to finish of the ride.

McTavish goes to a flying field in France, with Beery acting as chauffeur and Hatton as footman, both dressed in kilts, and McTavish curtsies.

Louise Brooks, a pretty little French girl, Mlle. Chelaine, of Chelaine's Carnival, comes to the field and asks the commanding officer for another balloonist, as she suspects the one they have, Malcolm Waite, is a German spy.

Ray makes a hit with Mlle. Chelaine and he and Wally become so upset by her beauty that they all most walk into an airplane, piloted by Duke Martin.

Duke starts to chase them and they run into an engine testing room where half a dozen engines are turning propellers at once. The clothes are blown off Beery and Hatton and an officer tosses them a couple of flying suits and tells them to beat it. They jump into a dummy plane to hide and find that the plane is on a wire and is lifted into the air to be used for target practice by the training planes.

When the dummy plane descends in flames Beery and Hatton jump out and run. They seek refuge in the Chelaine's carnival where they arrive just as Malcolm Waite is about to make a balloon jump. They get into a wardrobe wagon and outfit themselves in the carnival uniforms of white trousers, red coats and red and white caps.

The entire carnival company are then arrested as spies but Grisette tells the officers that Wally and Ray do not belong to the carnival, and that Waite is the spy. Waite is up in the balloon and Ray and Wally agree to capture him. They climb up into the basket and Waite cuts the balloon free and knocks them both senseless and jumps out.

Meanwhile the balloon drifts to earth. German troops now pursue them. They leap over a dead cow into a shell hole and draw the cow in after them. In a few minutes, camouflaged as the cow, they escape, to a German village.

The cow nearly collapses when Ray catches sight of a pretty girl—Griselle. She comes out to milk the cows and the fake cow ambles over to her. The fake cow leaves the barnyard in two sections when a German soldier appears. They are captured and taken to headquarters. Mean-

while, the maps and drawings made by Waite have been found in the balloon and Ray and Wally are suddenly hailed as heroes. Dressed in German uniforms and covered with medals, they are the toast of the populace, but they are little worried over the situation.

In a Chateau are Griselle and her mother, as Wally and Ray enter with the German officers. Wally, mistaking the girl for Grisette, asks her to walk with him. He is a hero and her mother urges her to go on. She asks Wally to kiss her. Ray sees this and tries to monopolize Griselle, who shrinks back toward Wally.

Ray shows Griselle the fan Grisette gave him. She sees the marking "Made in France," and in a fury, breaks it and turns to Wally and gives him a cheap vanity case marked "Made in Germany."

Word is brought that the Allies are about to attack and it is proposed to send Wally and Ray back to the front for some more of their clever spying. They are stunned, but are more stunned when they discover their pilot is to be Waite. Landing in France, they are arrested and sentenced to death as spies. Waite escapes and gets back to the carnival.

Grisette comes in and kisses Ray. Wally butts in and shows her the vanity case, and when she reads "Made in Germany," on it, she smashes it on the floor. Wally tells her he wishes she'd make up her mind which one she loves and she doesn't know what he's talking about.

Waite is captured and brought in and Grisette tells the officers he is a real spy. All decide they are spies, the officers give them a chance. They are to fly back over the German lines and one is to drop from a parachute as a signal for attack.

Once in the air Waite threatens to kill them both if they attempt the parachute drop. Wally taps Waite on the head with a wrench but when the plane goes into tail spins, he revives him and orders him to pilot it. Suspecting treachery, the French begin shooting at the plane, and Wally taps Waite on the head again and pushes him and the parachute overboard. Ray and Wally are arguing about who shall drive the plane and fail to see another plane ascend and write in smoke the word Armistice.

They nose-dive into no-man's land and they are surrounded by French and German soldiers. They think they are captured again but learn the war is over.

A month later they meet again at a French inn. Ray is married to Grisette, Wally is married to Griselle. The two brides cannot be told apart and when Ray sees Wally kissing Griselle he leaps at him. But Grisette enters just then and the tangle is straightened out and they all drink to happiness.

Erstwhile Army-Navy Boys Now Sailing Up

AVIATION, now the greatest popular fancy, has its comedy possibilities exploited for the first time in a motion picture by Wallace Beery and Raymond Hatton in "Now We're in the Air," the Paramount film which comes to the .... theatre ....

Against their will, Beery and Hatton have been soldiers, sailors and firemen, and now they are aviators, through no doing of their own. They land in the air service when their employer enlists and they wander into a propeller testing room and have their Scotch highlander costumes blown off.

Some one tosses them a pair of flying uniforms and before they know it they have been mistaken for aviators and are in the air. Mistaken identity dominates the plot. Louise Brooks plays a dual role. She is both of twin sisters, one of whom is of French reality and the other German. Beery falls in love with the German twin and Hatton with the French, but they are unable to tell the girls apart, so all sorts of scrambled complications ensue.

Then Beery and Hatton are mistaken for German heroes, and are acclaimed of the same status by the French. This is too good to last however, and they are about to be finished off by a firing squad when the war ends, and each wins the twin of his choice.

The picture is replete in thrilling aviation situations, but most of the comedy takes place on the ground. Clever gags punctuate the entire production and the picture may be safely said to be the funniest and best Hatton and Beery have done yet. Frank Strayer directed "Now We're in the Air," and the cast includes Malcolm Waite, Emile Chautard, Duke Martin and Russell Simpson.

Wind Machines Have Nothing on W. Beery

A battery of six wind machines, which create artificial cyclones with airplane propellers and airplane engines, was turned on Wallace Beery and Raymond Hatton for a scene of "Now We're in the Air," their new Paramount comedy now at the .... theatre.

The blast tore off their clothes and tossed them fifty feet into a net arranged to save them from injury.

"This is pie for me," said Beery, as he prepared to do the scene over again. "I was raised in Missouri where the wind really blows.

"Kansas cyclones have had lots of publicity, but those cyclones just use Kansas to get a running start. When they reach Missouri they're really traveling.

"I stepped out of our cyclone cellar once thinking the storm was over. The wind tossed me so far that it was four days before I got home. I wasn't hurt a bit because one of our straw stacks traveled along right under me and stopped when I did."

"I was raised in Iowa," said Hatton, "let me tell you about the wind storms there—

THE PRESS SHEET STORY

For each of its feature films, Paramount issued a Press Sheet, a multi-page publicity document covering various promotional angles. Meant for newspapers and magazines as well as the theaters set to show the film, it included all manner of background material as well as studio written profiles of the stars, director, and other key individuals associated with the production; typically, the Press Sheet also included a story synopsis, which is printed below. (A slightly longer version of the Press Sheet synopsis housed at the Margaret Herrick Library is credited to Beatrice Eleanor Carlisle, and dated August 5, 1927.)

# # #

Wallace Beery and Raymond Hatton are a couple of ship stokers who have been engaged as servants by Russell Simpson, who is a gouty old Scotchman, Lord Abercrombie McTavish. Simpson wants to enlist in the air service during the last year of the war. He visits a Flying Circus to see how altitude agrees with him. This makes him sure he can fly a plane but Beery and Hatton are terrified from start to finish of the ride.

McTavish goes to a flying field in France, with Beery acting as chauffeur and Hatton as footman, both dressed in kilts, and McTavish enlists.

Louise Brooks, a pretty little French girl, Mlle. Chelaine, of Chelaine's Carnival, comes to the field and asks the commanding officer for another balloonist, as she suspects the one they have, Malcolm Waite, is a German spy.

Ray makes a hit with Mlle. Chelaine and he and Wally become so upset by her beauty that they almost walk into an airplane, piloted by Duke Martin.

Duke starts to chase them and they run into an engine testing room where half a dozen engines are turning propellers at once. The clothes are blown off Beery and Hatton and an officer tosses them a couple of flying suits and tells them to beat it. They jump into a dummy plane to hide and find that the plane is on a wire and is lifted into the air to be used for target practice by the training planes.

When the dummy plane descends in flames Beery and Hatton jump out and run. They seek refuge in Chelaine's carnival where they arrive just as Malcolm Waite is about to make a balloon jump. They get into a wardrobe wagon and outfit themselves in the carnival uniforms of white trousers, red coats and red and white caps.

The entire carnival company are then arrested as spies but Grisette tells the officers that Wally and Ray do not belong to the carnival, and that Waite is the spy. Waite is up in the balloon and Ray and Wally agree to capture him. They climb up into the basket and Waite cuts the balloon free and knocks them both senseless and jumps out.

Meanwhile the balloon drifts to earth. German troops now pursue them. They leap over a dead cow into a shell hole and draw the cow in after them. In a few

minutes, camouflaged as the cow, they escape, to a German village.

The cow nearly collapses when Ray catches sight of a pretty girl—Griselle. She comes out to milk the cows and the fake cow ambles over to her. The fake cow leaves the barnyard in two sections when a German soldier appears. They are captured and taken to headquarters. Meanwhile, the maps and drawings made by Waite have been found in the balloon and Ray and Wally are suddenly hailed as heroes. Dressed in German uniforms and covered with medals, they are the toast of the populace, but they are little worried over the situation.

In a chateau are Griselle and her mother, as Wally and Ray enter with the German officers. Wally, mistaking the girl for Grisette, asks her to walk with him. He is a hero and her mother urges her to go. She asks Wally to kiss her. Ray sees this and tries to monopolize Griselle, who shrinks back toward Wally.

Ray shows Griselle the fan Grisette gave him. She sees the marking "Made in France," and in a fury, breaks it and turns to Wally and gives him a cheap vanity case marked "Made in Germany."

Word is brought that the Allies are about to attack and it is proposed to send Wally and Ray back to the front for some more of their clever spying. They are stunned, but are more stunned, when they discover their pilot is to be Waite. Landing in France, they are arrested and sentenced to death as spies. Waite escapes and gets back to the carnival.

Grisette comes in and kisses Ray, Wally butts in and shows her the vanity case, and when she reads "Made in Germany," on it, she smashes it on the floor. Wally tells her he wishes she'd make up her mind which one she loves and she doesn't know what he's talking about.

Waite is captured and brought in and Grisette tells the officers he is a real spy. All denying they are spies, the officers give them a chance. They are to fly back over the German lines and one is to drop from a parachute as a signal for attack.

Once in the air Waite threatens to kill them both if they attempt the parachute drop. Wally taps Waite on the head with a wrench but when the plane goes into tail spins, he revives him and orders him to pilot it. Suspecting treachery, the French begin shooting at the plane, and Wally taps Waite on the head again and pushes him and the parachute overboard. Ray and Wally are arguing about who shall drive the plane and fail to see another plane ascend and write in smoke the word Armistice.

They nose-dive into no-man's land and they are surrounded by French and German soldiers. They think they are captured again but learn the war is over.

A month later they meet again at a French inn. Ray is married to Grisette. Wally is married to Griselle. The two brides cannot be told apart and when Ray sees Wally kissing Griselle he leaps at him. But Grisette enters just then and the tangle is straightened out and they all drink to happiness.

"THE MILLION DOLLAR MYSTERY" and "SPLITTING THE BREEZE," COMPLETE IN THIS ISSUE.

BOY'S CINEMA

2d Every Wednesday

No. 454.
August 25th, 1928.

Weekly

"NOW WE'RE IN THE AIR"

WALLACE BEERY and RAYMOND HATTON in a Rousing Comedy.

BOY'S CINEMA WEEKLY

Boy's Cinema Weekly was just that, a once-a-week "every Wednesday" British periodical aimed at youth that featured short stories based on popular films. Today, the magazine is classified by librarians as either children's literature, or, belonging among the lowest of the low of popular fiction, the so-called "penny dreadfulls."

Boy's Cinema Weekly was begun in 1919 by Amalgamated Press in London, England. Notably, it included far more text than many of its English competitors. *Boy's Cinema Weekly* relied on the traditional short story form, whereas publications like *Film Fun* or *Kinema Comic* used illustrations and the comic strip to retell a film story.

Typically, the fictionalizations found in *Boy's Cinema Weekly* were adapted from war films, westerns, mysteries, crime stories or tales of adventure centering on heroic individuals like Houdini, Tarzan, Robinson Crusoe or Sherlock Holmes. Actors Buck Jones, Douglas Fairbanks, Lon Chaney and Strongheart (a canine film star) graced the magazine's cover at one time or another.

As this publication was aimed at boys, the stories featured in it centered on men and manly adventures. That may explain why Louise Brooks' twin characters, Griselle & Grisette, are barely mentioned in this prose retelling—despite their playing a central role in the film itself. One striking exception is the fleeting alliterative purple prose description of Grisette as a "Pleasant peasant and French wench"!

The *Boy's Cinema Weekly* fictionalization of *Now We're in the Air* appeared in the issue dated August 25, 1928. Because it was cheaply printed on pulpy paper, relatively few copies of this issue as well as most other issues have survived. Some, in fact, have grown scarce. (The author of this book has come across only two copies of the August 25th, 1928 issue. One is in his collection, while the other is housed in a bound volume at the British Library in London.)

This story, described as a "rollicking comedy of a comical pair, and their exciting adventures in the Air Force, which they join by force of circumstance," ran seven pages. It was "specially written" for the magazine based on "incidents in the new film *Now We're in the Air.*" No author is indicated.

Like the Spanish-language story which follows, this fictionalization was loosely adapted from the film. And just as *Now We're in the Air* can't claim to be great cinema, neither can these stories claim to be great literature.

" Now We're in the Air."

This is an amusing comedy of the war. It is screamingly funny, thoroughly exciting, and very good entertainment. The principal roles are taken by that irresponsible pair, Wallace Beery and Raymond Hatton, the heroes of "We're in the Navy Now," and "Fireman, Save My Child."

The cast of this comedy is as follows: Wally, Wallace Beery; Ray, Raymond Hatton; Grisette Chelaine and Griselle Chelaine, Louise Brooks; Angus McAllister, Russell Simpson; Professor Saenger, Malcolm Waite; Mons. Chelaine, Emile Chautard.

The teaser in *Boy's Cinema Weekly.*

A rollicking comedy of a comical pair, and their exciting adventures in the Air Force, which they join by force of circumstances.

Wallace Beery + Raymond Hatton in "NOW WE'RE IN THE AIR"

Trouble—in Kilts!

IT was on a bright November morning in the last year of the Great War that Wally McAllister, dressed in kilts, sat at the wheel of a hired car, driving at a great pace along the main road that runs out of Paris to the south.

Wally was a tall and bulky fellow, with a great, jolly face which was slightly disfigured at the moment by a pair of enormous horn-rimmed spectacles. The car was a ramshackle affair, and the engine was knocking, and the water in the radiator was nearly boiling; but Wally felt distinctly cold about the knees. In spite of his Scottish parentage this was the first time he had worn petticoats since his babyhood!

Beside him, also in kilts, sat his brother, Ray McAllister, a little shrimp of a fellow who made up for his lack of inches in his self-conceit. Wally could have picked him up in one hand, but Ray considered that he had the superior brain, and that without him his brother would be lost. Just now it seemed to him highly probable that the car would be smashed, and that they both would be killed—to say nothing of Angus McAllister, their uncle, who was being bounced about in his seat at the back.

Angus McAllister was a Scotsman from Scotland, proud of his clan, proud of his accent (which might have been cut with a knife), and fully convinced that the war could not be won without his assistance, although he was turned fifty, and suffered badly from gout. He had been rejected by the Army, the Navy and the Marines; but he had come to Paris with the aid of a friend in the War Office, determined to do something for his country. And he had decided that, since no other branch of the service would have him, he would get into the Air Force by hook or by crook.

"Even if a mon has got but one guid foot," he argued, "he can fly." But in Paris the Air Force wouldn't have anything to do with him. The British, the French, and the Americans all turned a deaf ear to his entreaties—the Americans were even rude to him.

Then Wally and Ray, his nephews, had arrived from New York.

Angus McAllister had money, and they had practically none at all. He had written to them, because he thought they might help him; and they had travelled across the Atlantic, risking submarines,

because they thought he might help them. And now, to please him, they were dressed in kilts and taking him to a big army flying school a number of miles south of Paris, where he hoped to persuade somebody that he was fit to become a hero in the air.

"Wally," bellowed Ray, "if you don't go slower I'll break your blessed neck before you have time to break all our blessed necks!"

"I can't go slower," retorted Wally, bending over the wheel and knocking his chilly knees together. "Uncle rented this car for an hour, and we've only got twenty-two minutes to go!"

"We shan't need them," declared Ray. "We shall go long before they're up!"

But no accident happened on the road. Accidents were to happen later—accidents which were to sweep these two into tremendous adventures, threaten them with all sorts of sudden death, and make heroes of them against their will. And Angus McAllister was to be left out of all these accidents and adventures, and to be rejected again with no one to drive him back to Paris! But, in spite of lorries that threatened to crash into them, and corners that loomed up and were negotiated on two wheels, they reached the aerodrome in safety.

The car swept off the road into a huge open field set about with hangars weirdly camouflaged with paint, dotted with officers and men, littered with sheds disguised as incredible haystacks with straw and paint. And here and there aeroplanes taxied across the grass, and here and there aeroplanes rose up into the sky.

Wally stopped the exhausted engine and brought the car to a standstill. Ray jumped down and opened the back door, and out clambered their irate uncle, full of gout and bad temper.

"I'd kill ye!" he cried angrily. "Kill the twa of ye—only ye're my nephews, and I'd have to pay for the hearse! Shakin' the life out o' me, ye bletherin' fools! Wha's ma stick!"

Wally and Ray plunged their heads and arms into the back of the car simultaneously in quest of the twisted stick their uncle needed as much as a lame

man needs a crutch. Both grasped it simultaneously, and the stick was more twisted than ever by the time Uncle Angus had snatched it from them.

He hobbled away without another word, but he gave them both a look that ought to have killed them on the spot.

Wally pulled his kilts down over his knees and glared at Ray.

"There he goes," he said. "Scotland's last hope! When he comes back rejected he'll be through with us for ever. What was that password you gave the sentry?"

"Rats," responded Ray. "As he was a Frenchman, and didn't understand it, he thought it must be right. It's brain that counts in these foreign lands. Pity you haven't got any, Wally!"

"Brain!" snorted Wally. "You little growing pain, you! It was your brain that thought of these kilts to please uncle! I'm frozen!"

"So am I," confessed Ray. "But we've come all the way from America to get uncle's million, and you've got to leave it to me, or he'll never leave it to us!"

An aeroplane whizzed over their heads, and Wally nearly fell backwards in his efforts to look up at it.

"Uncle must be part eagle," he said dismally, "wanting to go up there!"

"Part eagle? He's totally cuckoo!" declared Ray. "Mad right through! But if only they'd let him go up he'd break his neck, and then we'd be well off. Oh, look at that one!"

An aeroplane was humming through the air just above their heads, and they stepped backwards with their heads tilted upwards, watching its progress.

As they were looking where the aeroplane was going, they naturally didn't notice where they themselves were going. They bumped into the tail of a big machine which was standing on the grass. The tail dropped beneath the weight of Wally, and he rolled off.

The airman looked over the back of the cockpit, and saw them sitting on his tail. He was a big-faced man with china-blue eyes that glared at them from beneath his crash-helmet.

"Get out of it!" he yelled, and clambered out after them.

August 25th, 1928.

Trouble—Out of Kilts!

WALLY and Ray went off in haste, forgetting all about the car. And then, immediately before them, they saw a remarkably pretty girl, dressed like a French peasant, who was studying the remarkable evolutions of an aeroplane through a pair of field-glasses. She was standing on a little hillock.

"Rather a pleasant peasant, yon French wench—what?" said Wally, and he peered at her through his horn-rimmed spectacles.

Ray pushed him aside and advanced to the hillock.

"Good-morning!" he said, in very bad French. "How do you carry yourself?"

The girl looked at the little man with interest, and said something which Ray failed to understand.

Wally laughed scornfully.

"She wants to know why we are dressed like women!" he said. "Your brain may be better than mine, but your education's rotten. And it was your silly idea, anyway—so you can explain."

The girl had a fan in her left hand—though a fan is, to be sure, rather superfluous on a November day. She hit Ray on the wrist with it.

"Your frien'," she said, "he look silly!"

"Quite right," agreed Ray. "Go away, Wally!"

Wally refused to go.

"I don't look nearly as silly as you are!" he assured his brother. "What's your name, ma'moiselle?"

"Grisette," replied the girl. "But I don't like you!"

She turned to Ray.

"I give you my fan," she said, "for souvenir. You come to the circus—yes?"

"Circus?" exclaimed Ray.

"In field, over there. At two o'clock I perform. You come, is it not so?"

"Rather!" said Ray delightedly. "I wanted to make a date with you, as we call it in America."

She waved her hand to him and ran off. And Ray and Wally stood there waving to her till a shout from a uniformed mechanic caused them to look round. An aeroplane was taking-off across the field, and they were right in its path!

They ran; but, instead of running sideways, they ran straight ahead. The aeroplane bore down on them.

A little way ahead a flying officer was talking to three mechanics. The roar of the engine attracted their attention in the nick of time, and they scattered in all directions. Wally and Ray continued to run straight on!

The tip of the left wing caught them, flinging them to earth, and like a pair of startled rabbits they got to their feet and ran for cover.

A doorway yawned before them—the doorway of a huge shed that didn't look like a shed. They bolted into it.

It was a propeller-testing shed, and all around its walls were propellers, whizzing at so many thousand revolutions to the minute. The air in the middle of the shed was in such a state of agitation that their kilts were nearly torn off them, and their hair streamed upwards. They looked like a couple of clowns!

They grabbed at a rope because they could not keep on their feet, but they were swept away from the rope and cannoned into a switchboard which provided the current that caused the revolutions of the propellers.

There were wires on the switchboard —bare wires that gave them a tre-

August 25th, 1928.

mendous shock and flung them back into the whirlpool of air.

An officer on a little platform against the wall, ignoring their plight, issued an order to the man at the switchboard.

"Four hundred more revolutions!" he yelled.

The propellers whirled round faster than ever. Wally and Ray were swept into the middle of that awful air-current, and once more they clung to the rope that stretched across the shed. They were tossed this way and that, but they held on with all their might. Their feet went up into the air. Their clothes departed from their bodies, leaving them with nothing on but their vests and shorts. They gasped for breath. Their agonies were awful!

Then, it seemed, the officer in charge of the shed noticed them at last—or else the testing of the propellers was over. He bellowed an order; the propellers slowed down, the air became breathable and comparatively still. Wally and Ray snatched up their tattered garments and dived for the entrance, while the mechanics in charge of the propellers roared with delight.

The discomfited pair reached a doorway and rushed out. They made for some trees in the distance—and found themselves in the middle of a picnic party. France might be at war, but the Parisians must have their little amusements. There were some officers, some elderly Frenchmen, and some ladies in the party under the trees.

Wally stopped short with a cry of dismay and turned about. Ray followed him. They left the trees behind and reached a big tent of camouflaged canvas. Wally flung himself at the flap and rolled into the tent. Ray landed in the middle of his back.

"Did you see that airman?" gasped Ray.

"I did," admitted Wally. "That's why I popped in here. He seems to be annoyed with us for sitting on his tail. And he's ugly, too!"

"We can't go out like we are," decided Ray. "He's waiting for us."

Wally looked about him.

"It—it's a stores!" he exclaimed.

It was, more or less. There were wrenches and spanners and spare parts of all descriptions about them, and—most welcome of all—there were clothes! Not, to be sure, the sort of clothes they would have worn for preference, but, at least, clothes of a far more desirable character than the kilts they were clutching in their hands.

Blown Up.

FIVE minutes later they emerged from the tent arrayed as airmen— in overalls, jackets, crash-helmets, and goggles.

The big-faced fellow with the china-blue eyes was standing outside the tent, waiting for them, with a companion. He sprang to attention and saluted them, for he thought they were officers. But he didn't realise that these professional-looking figures were the kilted fools who had interfered with his machine.

But Wally and Ray had escaped from one danger only to run into another. A party of men, in training for the air service, came marching along, and a non-commissioned officer yelled to them to fall in.

They fell in, taking up their positions right in front of the squad, and marched across the field at a pace not strictly in accordance with regulations.

"Right turn!" roared the sergeant. And the squad obediently turned. But not Wally and Ray—they continued to march straight on.

"Halt!" howled the sergeant.

"Do we halt?" asked Wally doubtfully.

"Must!" responded Ray. "They might shoot!"

They halted, and the sergeant came up to them, breathing red fire. He called them all sorts of names that were not lawfully their own. Then he made them turn right, and eventually brought them into line with the other men. Wally blinked through his glasses at a number of aeroplanes ranged in a row on the grass in front of them.

"We chose the wrong clothes!" he groaned.

"Where are your parachutes?" bellowed the sergeant.

Wally looked at Ray. Ray looked inquiringly at the sergeant.

"Parachutes?" he echoed wonderingly.

"You'll be shot before the day's over!" thundered the sergeant. "Corporal—parachutes for these idiots!"

A corporal went off with two men, and presently returned with folded parachutes, which were strapped round the terrified pair.

"Remember your instructions," said the corporal. "If you get in trouble, pull the ring."

"Where's the ring?" asked Wally.

They showed him the ring, and then, the strapping being accomplished, the men returned to their respective positions.

"Bolt!" hissed Ray.

Wally bolted, with Ray beside him.

"Stop those men!" roared a flying officer who was talking to the sergeant. And immediately the sergeant, the corporal, and several of the men started off in hot pursuit.

"He said—pull the ring—if we're—in trouble," panted Ray. "We are, brother! Pull the ring!"

They found the rings as they ran, and tugged at them. The parachutes bellowed out behind them. Their feet deserted the hard ground; they seemed to be floating in the parachutes.

The officer and the sergeant blundered into the bulging material and rolled to the ground. The men stopped to laugh. Wally and Ray half-floated, half-ran into a big open space which, though they knew it not, was labelled:

"DANGER — BOMBING PRACTICE GROUND."

In the middle of this space there stood a shed which bore a board above its doorway; and on the board, in large black letters, was painted the forbidding notice:

"WARNING: NO ADMITTANCE."

They reached this shed.

"Cut your ropes!" cried Ray, and slashed at his own ropes with a knife which he had unexpectedly found in a pocket of his overalls.

Wally unfastened his ropes, and the parachutes fluttered to the grass. There came an explosion near by, and they clung to one another, then tumbled in at the doorway, and sat down on the floor of the shed.

"We're safe now, for a minute or two," said Ray.

But they were not safe even for ten seconds!

A hurricane of bombs struck the wooden walls of the shed and the ground round about it; there followed a series of explosions, and the shed went up into the air and came down in fragments!

Wally's head emerged from a litter of planks, and Wally's body slowly followed. There was a dazed expression on his face. He felt himself all over to make sure that no bones were broken.

"Thank goodness I'd taken my glasses off," he said to himself, "or they'd have been broken!"

Then he looked round for Ray, flinging boards and quarterings in all directions.

"Where are you, Ray?" he called anxiously. "You're too little to have been blown to bits, but you might tell a fellow if you're alive or dead!"

"I'm up in the attic," responded a feeble voice.

"Up in the—— You'd better come down, then!"

The voice of Ray seemed to have come from beneath the ground, and Wally began feverishly to clear away the debris from the spot.

His efforts disclosed a large hole, and out of this hole appeared Ray's face, considerably the worse for wear. Wally picked up the notice-board, which was lying intact beside him.

"Why didn't you see that before you led me into this?" he demanded. "Warning—No Admittance!"

"I didn't see it," complained his brother. "Help me out, you fool!"

Voices were shouting, and a number of men were running towards them. Wally, with a mighty heave, lifted Ray clean out of the hole, and together they made off as fast as their aching limbs would carry them.

At the Circus.

NOT more than a mile down the main road from the Flying School, the circus to which Grisette had referred occupied the major part of a large field. But though Grisette had called it a circus, her father, Monsieur Chelaine, who was its proprietor, called it something quite different—"Chelaine's Colossal Carnival," or French words to that effect.

There was a large balloon hovering over the tents and sideshows, held captive by ropes. Mons. Chelaine, wearing a large hat and a grandiose manner, was standing on a raised platform, introducing his daughter, Grisette, to the crowd that had gathered, when Wally and Ray looked curiously over a low wall and saw the girl who had given Ray her fan.

"We've come straight to the circus in time for the performance," cried Ray delightedly. "Look, Wally—she's going to dance!"

Grisette, as a matter of fact, was already dancing on the platform—dancing very gracefully, too.

The worthy pair passed in at a gateway and joined the crowd. The dance came to an end, and Mons. Chelaine reappeared.

"My daughter," he announced, "will now pass among you with her tambourine. Be generous, my friends!"

Presently Grisette drew near the two wanderers and stared in astonishment at their clothing.

"So you are *real* aviators?" she said.

Wally put his hand on his heart and bowed. Ray promptly gave him a push.

"Would you like to go up in our balloon?" asked Grisette.

"No!" they replied simultaneously and emphatically.

"I'd lots sooner go for a walk with you," declared Ray.

Over on the platform, Grisette's father was now introducing to the audience a big man in a top-hat and black cloak. His features were decidedly Teutonic, in spite of the monocle in his left eye.

"Professor Saenger, the fearless king of the air," announced Mons. Chelaine, "will now ascend, dressed just as he is, and descend from a dizzy height on a rope."

"Fancy anybody being impressed with that sort of thing while there's a war on and all those aeroplanes about," said Wally to Grisette.

"Yes," said Grisette, "we've chosen a bad spot. But, further south, we've been in villages where the people have hardly seen an aeroplane in their lives!"

Grisette's tambourine contained very little money as yet, and she seemed to have forgotten all about her task. Her father suddenly jumped down from the platform and stepped between her and Ray.

"I won't have you flirting with these aviators!" he cried, and drove his daughter away.

A number of men hauled down the balloon by its ropes, and Professor Saenger, with a great flourish, climbed into the basket. Then the balloon was released again to ascend as far as the ropes would permit.

"That's not much of a height to come down on a rope," remarked Wally scornfully. "Why, I went higher up than that just now, and came down on nothing! Wonder what he thinks he's doing up there?"

"Seems to be writing," said Ray.

As a matter of fact, Professor Saenger was not exactly writing up in the balloon—he was marking a map with the positions of various sections of the Army which were visible to him from that height!

Professor Saenger spoke French like a Frenchman, but he was in fact a German, and though Mons. Chelaine was a genuine showman and had engaged the fellow to do stunts, never dreaming that he was a spy, the professor was often able to supply information to the enemy.

Wally and Ray wandered off to look at some of the side-shows. They were watching a contortionist who seemed bent on tying his body into knots, when the big-faced airman with the china-blue eyes came round a caravan and caught sight of them. They backed in such haste that they bumped into a perpendicular board, and an instant later they jumped away from the board in still greater haste, because the points of two daggers came through and jabbed them in the back!

"What's happening?" gasped Ray.

They edged round either side of the board and found that a pretty girl in tights was standing there while a man in a white suit threw daggers into the board, making a pattern all round her.

"Oh," said Wally, "you're the Human Target, I suppose!"

The girl smiled.

"Mind he doesn't hit you!" urged Ray. "It's very dangerous!"

Wally had inadvertently leant forward, so that his head was in the way of the marksman. A dagger whizzed past the back of his neck and buried itself

They emerged from the tent arrayed as airmen.

August 25th, 1928.

in the board. Another dagger struck the board within an inch of Ray's nose.

They fled. And as they fled the airman pursued. At first he had been a little uncertain as to their identity; now he was sure of it.

The worthy pair dodged in and out among the caravans till their pursuer was out of sight. Then they crept into a small tent which was used as a dressing-room.

The tent was deserted.

"Exchange is no robbery!" cried Ray, and pounced on some blue-grey French uniforms hanging on a peg.

They emerged, a few minutes later, looking something like a pair of French officers, though, to be sure, Wally's uniform was an exceedingly tight fit, whereas Ray's was as loose on him as the skin is on a rhinoceros!

Two real French officers were standing near the tent talking sternly to Mons. Chelaine.

"Ever since this circus arrived," declared one of them, "the enemy air raids have been more successful. Your credentials are in order, but evidently there's a spy in your troupe."

Grisette stole up to Ray, staring at the uniform he was wearing.

"What do these officers from the aviation school want?" she whispered. "Are they looking for deserters?"

Ray made a grimace, and Wally answered hurriedly in a loud voice:

"They say there's a spy in disguise with your circus."

Grisette looked at her father and frowned. Then she addressed the two officers.

"The man you want," she said, "is up in that balloon, then. I'm sure of it—he carries maps and things about with him."

The officers thanked her, and issued orders. The men in charge of the ropes were told to haul the balloon down.

Professor Saenger, finding himself descending, looked over the side of the basket and began to swear fluently—in German!

"Hear that!" cried Wally.

The professor, in a fury, began to unfasten the sand-bags that hung round the basket, dropping them on the heads of the men below. One fell on Ray and burst, smothering him with sand.

In the Air.

BY this time the balloon was only a few feet from the ground, and Wally jumped at it, caught hold of the edge of the basket and clambered in. Ray, with a flying leap, followed him. The professor took a knife from his pocket and slashed at the ropes. Up went the balloon again, all its ropes severed save two, and to these two a couple of men were clinging desperately.

The professor flung off his cloak and coat and sprang at the intruders, but Wally was ready for him, and, with a mighty heave, tumbled him over the side on to the crowd beneath. Wally looked down after him. There was a rope ladder hanging down from the side of the basket.

"They've got him," he said; "and I'm going to get back on the ground before this balloon goes up in the air."

He had got his feet on the rungs of the swaying ladder, and was descending in haste when a cry from Ray caused him to look down. The two men had let go of the remaining ropes, and the balloon was soaring upwards! There was a sheer drop of fully seventy feet between the end of the ladder and the earth!

Wally climbed up again in a panic, and Ray helped him into the basket.

The balloon drifted with the wind over fields and lanes and camps. Wally

and Ray crouched in the basket, wondering what on earth to do. There were two sandbags left, and after a while they removed them from their hooks. Ray had remembered that the professor had thrown down ballast, and suggested that they should do the same.

Naturally the balloon rose still higher! Wally shook his massive fist at his diminutive brother.

"You little molecule!" he roared. "I'll give you two minutes to think of something better!"

But Ray couldn't think of anything at all. He examined the basket anxiously, and he pulled open a trap-door in the bottom of it, through which he nearly fell. Then he said dismally:

"It's no good, I don't understand balloons."

They were crossing a broad river by this time, on the far side of which was a sandy bank, fringed with trees. A cow was standing near the edge of the water. In a lane near by a column of German infantry came marching along.

"Germans!" gasped Ray, who was looking down.

Wally peered down through his glasses; the soldiers looked up. There was a gun with the column, and evidently the officer in charge gave instructions, for the column halted, and the gun was trained on the balloon.

"They're going to shoot us down!" gasped Ray.

"There's something the matter with that cow!" exclaimed Wally, who was looking the other way.

And there certainly was. It had walked up the bank towards the clump of trees, and now, even as Wally watched, its body parted in the middle, and a man emerged from each half, dropped the pieces of carcase on the grass, and made off into the coppice.

"Spies!" shouted Wally. "Jolly good stunt!"

"It's a gun, you idiot!" cried Ray. "They're just going to fire!"

There followed a flash and a roar, and then a shell shot past the heads of the frightened pair, and they found themselves clinging to the basket at a grotesque angle. All the stay-ropes but two had been shot away!

There came another flash, another roar, followed by an explosion above their heads. The envelope of the balloon was in flames!

Necessity sharpens wits! The basket was dropping earthwards like a stone, and Ray was clinging to Wally, thinking his last moment had come, when Wally noticed for the first time a thing hanging on the edge of the basket that looked somehow familiar. It had a ring, and he grabbed with both hands at the ring. It was a parachute!

The basket dropped from beneath their feet, shot and shell seemed to rage all about them. But now they were floating—floating away from their enemies, towards the river, and descending gently through the air.

Presently the belt of trees hid them from the Germans, and they came to rest upon the sandy bank.

"What d'you mean by hanging on to me like that?" demanded Wally, indignantly. "You were nearly choking me!"

"You wouldn't have saved my life if I hadn't," said Ray. "Was it brains or accident that made you grab this parachute?"

"Brains!" declared Wally. "Let's hop it!"

They scrambled up the bank. They could hear the sound of running feet and eager cries in German.

"The cow!" cried Wally. And he led the way to the spot where he had seen

the spies discard the papier-maché contrivance.

Ray picked up one of the pieces and examined it.

"You have got some brains," he said grudgingly. "We'll hide inside it. I'll be the front end and you be the hind end."

"You can't make a cow's hind-end out of me!" objected Wally.

There was no time for argument, so Wally wriggled into the front portion and Ray slipped into the back. Then they united the contrivance in the middle and stood there, because five German soldiers were approaching.

"Where would you go if you were a cow?" inquired Wally from inside his end of the animal.

"Into the water," said Ray from his end.

Wally found that there was a peep-hole in the chest of the contrivance, and he turned in the direction of the water. The soldiers passed by unsuspectingly. Ray, who had found a little door in the flanks of the arrangement, peered out through it with considerable satisfaction.

"Saved!" he exclaimed. "Now what do we do?"

"Better go on being a cow," suggested Wally. "We'll get up into the roadway and see if we can find our way out of the hands of the enemy."

The Adventures of a "Cow"!

THEY reached the road and wandered along it, looking more or less like a real cow, for the papier-maché model had been very cleverly made. But they turned in the wrong direction. Though they knew it not, they were in Alsace, a considerable number of miles from the nearest French outpost.

Now Grisette Chelaine had come from Alsace, travelling with her father and the circus; but her mother, who had been born in Berlin and had German sympathies, had remained behind in the pleasant house where Grisette was born, and with Madame Chelaine remained Grisette's twin sister, Griselle.

The Germans had come soon after the circus had departed, and Madame Chelaine had welcomed the chance to serve her countrymen. A German general and his officers were using the house as their headquarters. The village was alive with troops. Griselle hated it all, but what could she do? The enemy were in occupation, and at least she and her mother were treated kindly.

General Schwartz, the officer commanding, was at dinner in the pleasant farm-house, when Wally and Ray, in the guise of a brown cow, reached the village street. So far they hadn't met a soul, but now a whole platoon of German soldiers was approaching.

"Look out!" said Wally warningly.

Ray opened the little door near his head and looked out in a literal sense. He shivered.

"What shall we do?" he gasped.

"Get inside," grunted Wally, "and goose-step when we pass—that'll make 'em think we're a cow of their own nationality."

The soldiers came on; the cow goose-stepped past them, much to the amusement of the men. And then, just as the immediate danger seemed to be over, a dog ran out and barked round the heels of the remarkable animal, scenting men within its carcase!

Wally kicked, Ray kicked. But the dog retreated, only to return, snapping and sniffing.

There was a wide gateway beside the road—the gateway of the farmhouse where Griselle and her mother lived—where General Schwartz was sitting at table in the living-room surrounded by his officers.

Wally and Ray made for the gateway and entered. There was a cowshed in the yard, and they made for that, too. A German sentry drove the dog away with his bayonet. The "cow" plunged into the cowshed and pulled up beside a real cow.

"We're in a hole now," whispered Ray hoarsely.

"We're in a cowshed," whispered Wally. "As soon as it's dark we'll get out again."

But Wally was rather too much of an optimist. It so happened that General Schwartz was a teetotaller, and liked a glass of milk with his meals. He turned to his orderly and said:

"Go, find a cow, and get me some fresh milk!"

The orderly went out into the farmyard, demanded a pail from a sergeant who was stationed there, and marched across to the shed.

He was a very mild-looking orderly, with a pair of spectacles on his nose. A very short-sighted orderly.

He approached the cow which really consisted of Wally and Ray, and he placed the pail beneath the "animal's" body. Then he picked up some hay and offered it to the mouth at Wally's end.

"Commence!" said the orderly in German. (As may be gathered, he knew nothing whatever about the milking of cows.)

"What do we do?" whispered Ray.

It was an awkward situation. Wally decided that the only thing to do was to frighten the orderly away. So suddenly he lifted up his voice and bellowed:

"*No milk to-day!*"

The orderly jumped as though he had been shot, and rushed blindly from the shed. He burst into the presence of the general.

"The cow spoke!" he cried wildly. "The cow spoke!"

"What!" cried General Schwartz. "Arrest the cow and bring it here!"

The "cow" was trying to sneak out of the yard into the road when a number of soldiers pounced upon it. A

struggle followed, in the course of which the two pieces fell apart, and Wally and Ray were revealed to the astonished gaze of the Germans. They were dragged forth from their place of concealment and marched into the house, prisoners.

Now, in the course of that terrible experience in mid-air, when the gun had shot away the ropes of the balloon and set fire to the envelope, most of the clothing of Wally and Ray had been torn to shreds, but by some stroke of fortune the professor's coat had become entangled with the parachute, and Wally, on reaching terra firma, had put it on. It didn't suit him, but at least it more or less fitted him, the professor being also a bulky man.

"You can speak their language," whispered Wally, as they were bundled over the threshold of the farmhouse, "but what'll *I* do?"

"Pretend to be deaf and dumb," replied Ray, in an undertone. "Concentrate on the deafness—your dumbness is perfect."

They found themselves in the raftered living-room, facing a big table spread with good things.

They were both feeling hungry, but the sight of all the German faces round the table made them forget their appetite. They glanced back. Their captors had retired after thrusting them into General Schwartz's presence. They dived for the doorway, but two soldiers who were standing on either side of it immediately barred their way, and the door closed with a crash.

General Schwartz glowered at them.

"So here is the cow, eh?" he grunted. "Search them!"

The two soldiers proceeded to search them, and—much to Wally's surprise—from the pocket of the black coat he was wearing a large folded map was produced.

This was handed over to the general, who inspected it with interest.

Suddenly he jumped to his feet with an exclamation.

"This is the map we've been expecting!" he cried.

Wally and Ray looked at one another open-mouthed. The general beamed on them.

"I'm proud that our secret service has two such brilliant fellows," he exclaimed delightedly, rising to his feet.

All the officers round the table stood up and raised their glasses in the direction of the two extraordinary figures near the door.

"Hick! Hick!" said Ray. "I mean: 'Hock! Hock!'"

The officers drank, and then left the table to shake the two heroes by the hand.

Madame Chelaine and her daughter Griselle came in at the door from the kitchen bearing heavily-laden trays.

"What's the old boy saying?" whispered Wally.

The "old boy"—otherwise the general —was saying:

"We are going to give a banquet in honour of you two heroes."

But Ray translated it into three whispered words:

"Eats for us!"

Then his eyes encountered Griselle's beautiful face and he gasped.

"Grisette!" he murmured.

Wally looked across the room, and at that moment Griselle looked at him —and smiled.

He smiled back at her, but Ray scowled, for a young German subaltern was showing her a paper. Ray couldn't see the paper, but it was an illustrated one, and he was pointing to the picture of a girl in dancing costume.

"So you are a dancer?" said the subaltern.

But Griselle shook her head.

"No," she said. "That is Grisette, my twin sister. We are exactly alike, but she went with papa and his circus before the war broke out, and they are in France."

The Death Sentence.

WALLY and Ray heard none of this conversation, and very naturally imagined Griselle to be Grisette, since the two girls were exactly alike. They would have moved across to her, but just then the general suggested that they should have a wash and change of raiment, and the orderly escorted them to another room.

Ten minutes later they returned to the living-room in German uniforms, looking singularly clean and smart, and feeling very hungry.

WARNING NO ADMITTANCE

" Why didn't you see that before you led me into this?" he demanded.

August 25th, 1923.

"Remember, 'dumb's' the word!" whispered Ray. "I'll do the talking. Hallo, there's my little French pastry again!"

Griselle had just appeared with food for the pair, and the pair went over to her together. Ray kissed her. She couldn't prevent him from doing so because she was encumbered with the tray; but she looked indignant.

"You remember me?" said Ray in German.

"I've never met you before," she retorted, "and I prefer your friend!"

Wally didn't understand what she said, but there was no mistaking the smile she gave him. Ray was furious.

They took their places at the table and did full justice to the food that was placed before them. And they were drinking their coffee when a young officer came in, saluted, and approached General Schwartz, to whom he made a lengthy report.

The general stood up.

"The Americans have taken over this sector," he said. "We need information as to their strength. I want two volunteers to get behind the American lines."

Ray translated this in a low voice for Wally's benefit.

"This is our chance to get away," he said. "Stand up!"

Wally obediently stood on his feet, and Ray stood beside him.

"We'll be delighted to get behind the American front, sir," he said in German.

"Splendid!" exclaimed General Schwartz. "Gentlemen, charge your glasses and drink to these noble fellows!"

Griselle jumped on to a chair to toast them, and she blew kisses to Wally.

Once more the two were escorted to another room, where they were provided with garments such as are worn by French peasants.

"They think of everything, don't they?" said Wally, regarding with disfavour the things he had now to put on.

When they were dressed they were escorted to a waiting car, in which they were whizzed off to a hangar, where an aeroplane was standing in readiness for departure. The pilot was already in his seat.

Wally and Ray climbed nimbly in, and then came a shock! The lieutenant who had accompanied them leaned over the side and spoke.

"When you get up," he said, "if you find the Americans unprepared, jump from the 'plane with your parachutes as a signal for us to attack."

"What did he say?" whispered Wally. Ray explained.

"So this is our chance to escape!" Wally groaned. "You're a clever little fool, aren't you?"

The lieutenant stared.

"What did your dumb comrade say?" he inquired.

"Fritz," said Ray, "you know the sign language—talk to him!"

Wally made a variety of unintelligible signs and motions with his hands and head.

"He regrets," translated Ray, "that he has only one neck to give for the Fatherland!"

The machine took off, sailed up into the air, circled round, and then flew north-east. It passed over No-Man's-Land, through skies torn with storm and shrapnel. Anti-aircraft guns belched at it.

There was no opportunity for any

parachute descent! With one of the wings badly damaged, the German airman made the best landing he could behind the American lines. The Americans were far from unprepared!

Within twenty minutes of starting out upon the journey, therefore, Wally and Ray were marched into the presence of a lieutenant of the American Flying Service, in a room in a hut near the Flying School.

"A big 'plane came down behind our lines," reported the sergeant who had brought them in. "These two spies jumped out, and the machine managed to get away."

"Right-ho!" said the lieutenant cheerfully. "I'll give them a fair trial and then hang them."

"Here, I say——" began Ray in alarm. But he broke off with a start, for into the room stalked the big-faced airman with the china-blue eyes. He strode round to the back of the table, which was in the middle of the room, and glared at them. Then, waggling a menacing finger at them, he cried:

"So you two are back again!"

"We—er—we were just out for the ride——" Wally stammered.

"You'll take your next ride in a hearse!" snapped the airman. "Lieutenant, I can tell you quite a lot about these fellows, and nothing to their credit." And he proceeded to relate how they had made themselves a nuisance in the morning; how they had disguised themselves at frequent intervals, sought the circus, and escaped to the German lines in the balloon.

"Oh, we'll have them shot at once," decided the lieutenant. "Take them away!"

The door opened, and a captain stepped into the room. He stared at Wally and Ray. He looked round at the junior officers and two men, who were standing to attention.

"What's this?" he asked sternly.

"Spies, sir," said the lieutenant. "I've just sentenced them."

The captain scowled.

"You have exceeded your authority," he snapped. "I'll handle this matter myself."

He dropped his gloves as he spoke, and immediately Wally and Ray were struggling with one another on the floor to pick them up.

Wally secured them and presented them with a flourish. Ray, not to be outdone in politeness, swung round the revolving-chair which the lieutenant had vacated directly the captain had entered the room.

"Thanks!" said the captain. But as he went to sit, the chair continued to revolve, and he landed on the floor with a thud.

He rose up, boiling with rage.

"Take them away," he cried, "and execute them at sunrise—rain or shine!"

"Yessir," said the sergeant.

Ray and Wally dodged, but the airman seized them with a triumphant chuckle, and was bundling them towards the door when once more it opened. A major entered, and as he entered, the airman cannoned right into him with his prisoners.

The airman jumped back and saluted.

"What's this?" bellowed the major.

"Spies, sir," said the captain. "I've just sentenced them."

The major looked Wally and Ray up and down. They bowed humbly.

"You have exceeded your authority, captain," said the major sternly. "I'll handle this affair."

"L-let me get you a chair, sir," said

Wally eagerly, and he moved the revolving chair towards the officer.

"Thank you," said the major, and went to sit down. But the big-faced airman, afraid that the two might be let off, lifted the top of the chair from its legs—and the major sat down on the legs, whence he rolled to the floor, swearing.

"Let someone get a chair that knows how to got a chair!" he barked.

The airman, who had hurriedly put the chair together again, pushed it forward and held it. The major sat down.

"Have these things shot!" he cried contemptuously. And waved his hand.

"Right away, sir?" asked the airman hopefully.

"No—at dawn!" was the reply.

Wally and Ray looked anxiously at the door, hoping that a general would appear. But no such thing happened, and the unlucky pair were dragged away and shut up in a barn for the night with a guard outside the door. It was a dreadful night!

"Anyway," said Wally gloomily, just before dawn, "we had a pretty full day yesterday—and we travelled a lot."

"We'll travel a lot farther this morning!" groaned Ray. "Why did uncle want to enlist?"

"I'd be a little happier if they shot him at the same time," said Wally. "He brought all this on us!"

Reprieved.

AT about half-past six in the morning the two captives were brought forth from their place of confinement and marched across a field to the long garden wall of a neighbouring chateau.

The wall was concreted between its stone buttresses, and they were left facing it. They stared at the patch of concrete.

More or less on a level with Ray's head and Wally's heart were a number of little round black marks, and several of the marks were adorned with pencilled crosses, arrows, and inscriptions. Ray examined a mark round which a heart had been outlined.

"What's all this mean?" he said quaveringly to Wally.

Wally pointed to some of the roughly written words:

"Boche," "Hun spy," "Good shot," "Five spies," and so on.

"They're where the bullets hit the wall," he said. "Wonder what they'll chalk up about us!"

"'Bout turn!" bellowed a voice.

They turned about to find that they were facing a firing-squad.

"Are we in your way?" inquired Wally.

The men laughed, the rifles of the firing squad wavered, and the pair promptly darted farther along the wall. But the captain and the major and the blue-eyed airman, who had come out to see them shot, dashed after them and dragged them back.

The airman was holding Wally, and the captain was clutching Ray, when the caravans of "Chelaine's Colossal Carnival" came rumbling along the road near by. Mons. Chelaine had been ordered to pack up and depart, and was departing.

Grisette was sitting in front of one of the caravans when she caught sight of the prisoners.

"Stop! Stop!" she cried out, and jumping down from her seat she rushed across the field.

Wally broke away to greet her, but she ignored him and went up to Ray. Ray shook off the captain's hands.

"Say, Grisette," he exclaimed, "I wish you'd make up your mind which of us it is you like before we're shot!"

"Shot?" she echoed in alarm. Then she turned to the major.

"These men are not spies!" she cried. "Your soldiers have just caught the real spy in the field over there we've just left. His 'plane was forced down, and he's been lurking there all night."

"Hold these fellows!" exclaimed the major, and started off towards the roadway. Grisette nestled in Ray's arms.

But the respite was a very brief one. Already a party of soldiers were dragging the German airman across the field, and they met the major half-way.

"Put him with the other two against that wall!" ordered the major.

But the German airman, on catching sight of Wally and Ray, protested vehemently.

"Those are the men you want!" he declared. "I'm only the pilot of the machine—they are the master minds."

"Shoot the lot of them!" ordered the major.

The whole three were being ranged in a row against the wall when a car drove up. The door opened and a general descended from it. Everybody saluted and stood to attention.

"What's all this?" demanded the general.

"Spies, general," responded the major. "I've been trying to shoot them all morning."

The general looked at Wally and Ray, who were standing against the wall with their fingers in their ears. Then he looked at the German airman, who had been placed a little farther along. He glared at the major.

"You have exceeded your authority, major," he said. "I'll handle this matter."

He strode over to Wally and Ray.

"Take your fingers out of your ears and tell me what it's all about," he commanded.

Wally launched into a lengthy account of the adventures which had befallen them, while Ray tried to get in a word edgeways, but without success.

"And that German pilot over there," wound up Wally, "brought us over to find out how strong your lines were——"

"Yes," broke in Ray, "and if you aren't strong, we're to go back and signal by making a parachute drop!"

The general stroked his chin.

"H'm," he decided, "you boys are much too valuable to shoot. Major, send the firing party away! Come with me, boys. And, captain, bring that Hun airman over to the hangar."

The whole party marched off across the field to an aeroplane.

"Get in," said the general to Wally and Ray. "We're prepared for any attack. You're to fly back with your pilot and make that parachute drop!"

"Please——" began Wally pitifully. But they bundled him into the machine and bundled Ray in after him.

"Give them parachutes," ordered the general. "And instruct the pilot."

The German clambered into the cockpit. The general leaned over and said to him in German:

"You will take this machine back to your own lines." Then he said in English to Wally and Ray: "And you two will make that parachute jump, or our escort 'planes will blow you out of the air!"

In the Air Again.

THE machine taxied across the field and rose into the air. And as it rose, two other machines rose up, one on either side of it. The general was taking no chances!

Down in the field the general watched the flight of the aeroplanes through a pair of glasses, and near an armoured car containing an anti-aircraft gun, Grisette did the same.

The three aeroplanes soared into the sky and swept off towards the German lines. Guns began to roar.

"If one of us doesn't jump," shouted Ray in Wally's ear, "those birds will start shooting, too!"

But the pilot suddenly stood up and swung round, and levelled a revolver at them.

"Let them shoot!" he bellowed, stopping his engines. "I won't send my countrymen into that trap!"

"Let's jump!" urged Ray. "They say that after the first bounce you don't feel a thing!"

The revolver threatened.

"Throw those parachutes overboard!" roared the pilot. "And then jump if you want to!"

There was no help for it. Over went the two folded parachutes, and down they fell likes stones.

The pilot sat down again and re-started the engines. His unwelcome passengers were helpless now; he would fly back to his own people, risking destruction!

But Wally suddenly noticed a spanner lying on the seat beside him. He snatched it up, kissed it, and brought it down with all his might on the back of the German's neck!

The fellow pitched forward, stunned. Wally reached over, grabbed at the revolver, and levelled it.

"You've got a parachute strapped to you," he yelled. "Jump, or I'll blow your blessed brains out!"

The German might, perhaps, have put up some sort of resistance if he had been in full possession of his senses; but, still dazed from the blow and threatened by the revolver, he got up on to the seat and jumped.

For some distance he fell at an appalling speed, then the parachute opened, and he went sailing down—towards the American lines.

"They've given the signal!" cried the general delightedly. "Start the attack!"

The attack started. Guns of all sizes and calibres suddenly lifted up their horrible voices.

The aeroplane pitched and tossed.

"The French are after us!" shrieked Ray.

The German guns began to reply.

"The other guys are after us, too!" shrieked Wally.

The aeroplane's tail went down, and the machine began a terrifying tail-dive.

Wally, who had pitched over into the pilot's seat, desperately grabbed at one of the controls to avoid being flung overboard, and fortune favoured the pair. He happened to grab at the right control. The tail came up, the dive ended, and the machine flattened out and went sailing gracefully towards the earth.

It crashed into a shed, flinging Wally and Ray forth on to a patch of blackened turf. They sat up and rubbed their heads.

"Where are we?" gasped Wally.

Then an extraordinary thing happened —a thing far more extraordinary than anything that had happened yet. The firing suddenly ceased; a dead silence succeeded all the din. And then, out from the trenches form either side of No-Man's-Land swarmed soldiers of all nationalities, flinging their rifles into the air, and shouting joyfully.

"It's the end of the world!" exclaimed Ray, aghast.

"No; it's the end of the war!" yelled Wally. "Look, Ray! Look!"

An aeroplane high up in the sky had just completed the writing of a single word in smoke. The word was:

"ARMISTICE."

All Aboard!

NEVER having been in the Army officially, Wally and Ray were the very first two to get out of it. Indeed, they got out with honours!

They went back to Paris, and there they saw their Uncle Angus. He had been rejected, as before, but since the war was over and his gout was a lot better, he was in quite a good temper, and even gave them money.

A fortnight later they set out in search of Grisette, and since it was fairly easy to follow the tail of a circus, they eventually caught up with it on the borders of Alsace. And then, of course, from Grisette's lips they learned the truth—that she was in love with Ray, and that the girl who had seemed to favour Wally was her twin-sister, Griselle.

The circus was making for the farm-house in Alsace, now that the war was over, and Mons. Chelaine suggested that the two brothers should travel with it.

But while Ray readily agreed to this, Wally declined. He was in haste to find Griselle. He remembered that young German subaltern, who had seemed to be paying her attention. So he hired a car, and hurried on to the farmhouse. And there he found Griselle and her mother. The Germans had departed.

By the time the circus arrived, Wally and Griselle had become engaged, and a double wedding followed a few weeks later in the little village church.

The two couples spent their honeymoons apart, but they met again, by arrangement, at Cherbourg, on the liner which was to carry them to New York.

Grisette walked up the gangplank carrying a French poodle, followed by Ray. And these two had hardly reached the deck before Griselle appeared with a dachshund—and Wally.

The crowd of passengers who were streaming aboard parted the two husbands from their wives, and they rushed about looking for them.

Ray, just as the boat began to move, came upon Wally kissing Grisette, and stalked angrily up to him.

"From now on," he cried, "you will please salute my wife only by raising your hat in the usual way!" And he thrust himself between them.

"What do you mean—your wife?" demanded Wally. "She's my wife!"

"We don't want the trouble we had in Alsace all over again," said Ray. "We married twins, and that makes us brothers-in-law as well as brothers. But my wife is my wife, not yours—and this is my wife!"

Just then Griselle came round the corner of a deck cabin and darted forward.

"I thought I'd lost you, Wally," she said, in broken English.

Wally looked at her, and then looked at Grisette. He scratched his head.

"My wife looks more like yours than yours does," he groaned. "What shall we do about it?"

Ray patted himself on the chest.

"I always deliver the big idea," he said proudly. "We can tell them apart by their dogs!"

(Specially written for the BOY'S CINEMA, by permission of Famous-Lasky Film Service, Ltd., from incidents in the new film, "Now We're in the Air," starring Wallace Beery as Wally and Raymond Hatton as Ray.)
August 25th, 1928.

Now We're in the Air

Paramount Famous Lasky Corp.
1927

Restored 2017
Národní filmový archiv
San Francisco Silent Film Festival

SAN FRANCISCO
SILENT
FILM FESTIVAL

Národní
filmový
archiv

NOW WE'RE IN THE AIR was produced by
Paramount Famous Lasky Corp. and released 22 October 1927.
The original American length was six reels (1,767 meters).

This restoration is based on the only known surviving element, an
incomplete 35mm tinted nitrate print (552 meters) that includes
portions of the original reels 2, 3, and 6. The print has Czech
intertitles and is preserved at the Národní filmový archiv
(National Film Archive) in Prague, Czech Republic.

New English intertitles have been created for this restoration.
The new titles are based on the original Paramount continuity
script which is conserved at the Margaret Herrick Library.
These new titles feature the same Paramount logo frame and
use a typeface similar to the Czech titles they replace.

The color tinting reproduces the original color scheme
that is indicated in the script.

Intervals of three seconds of black frames indicate the
transition between each of the sections.

This restoration was completed in May 2017 as a
partnership between the Národní filmový archiv
and the San Francisco Silent Film Festival.

A selection of images from the preserved fragment of *Now We're in the Air*.
Courtesy of the San Francisco Silent Film Festival

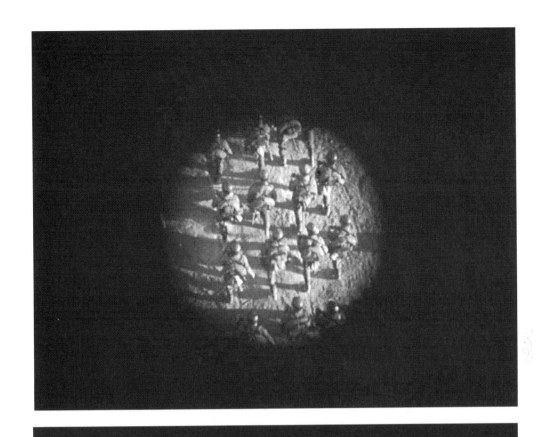

Restoration
Robert Byrne

Národní Filmový Archiv
Michal Bregant
Veroslav Haba

Research and Continuity
Thomas Gladysz
Christy Pascoe

Grading and 35mm Negative
Haghefilm Digitaal
Gerard de Haan

35mm Printing
Library of Congress

35mm Color Tinting
Jan Ledecký
Karel Wagner

Special Thanks
Kevin Brownlow
Louise Brooks Society
Margaret Herrick Library
Mike Mashon

LA NOVELA PARAMOUNT

Reclutas
en los
aires

Wallace Beery

Raymond Hatton

Louise Brooks

25 CTS

LA NOVELA PARAMOUNT

Like *Boy's Cinema Weekly* in England and the well known *Le Film complet* in France, Spain's *La Novela Paramount* was one of a number of European publications devoted, in whole or in part, to short fictionalizations of current films.*

Essentially a sub-genre of the fan magazine, such publications specialized in a narrative retelling of a film story—often with movie stills added. Some of these publications were aimed at a particular audience or aligned with a particular genre, like romance or adventure stories, while others were tied to a particular studio. Such was the case with *La Novela Paramount*, which was tied to Paramount Films and its regional distributor, Paramount S.A.

La Novela Paramount was published by Edicione Bistange in Barcelona, one of the leading publishers of film magazines on the Iberian Peninsula. (Remarkably, there were dozens of short and long-lived film story magazines in Spain in the 1920s, including the Edicione Bistange-published *La Novela MGM*, *Films de Amor*, *La Novela Cinematographica del Hogar* and others.) *La Novela Paramount* was among the shorter-lived magazines. Published in 1927 and 1928, *La Novela Paramount* ran 88 issues.

The issue devoted to *Reclutas en Los Aires* was published in 1928, as number 62. The publication cost 25 centavos, and measured approximately 4 x 6 inches, or 10.5 x 15.5 centimeters. *Reclutas por Los Aires* is described as a "chispeante comedia," a lively or sparkling comedy.

No author is indicated. The story ran 30 pages, filling most all of this ephemeral 32 page publication.

---

* In the United States, similar magazines included *Moving Picture Stories*.

RECLUTAS POR LOS AIRES

Argumento de la película

Esta película está dedicada a los valientes aviadores que lucharon por la libertad del aire para toda clase de aves, con excepción de las de corral.

Estamos en plena guerra europea. En la escuela de aviación de los alrededores de París los futuros "ases" se aprestaban a afrontar toda clase de enemigos aéreos.

Cierta mañana llegaron en automóvil al campo de aviación tres sujetos de extraña indumentaria con faldellines a la escocesa.

Eran el señor Angus y dos sobrinos, llamados Wally y Ray.

El tío se había empeñado en ser aviador a pesar de lo que, los dos brazos del ejército, a saber, el terrestre y el marítimo, le habían desechado por inútil.

Wally y Ray habían venido de América para acompañar a su tío Angus en la famosa aventura.

Pero, también en la aviación rechazaron al eterno aspirante por ser demasiado viejo, y Wally y Ray no pudieron contener su risa ante el fracaso.

—Si no fuese porque sois mis sobrinos y tendría que pagaros el entierro, os mataría a los dos ahora mismo... — gritó Angus, furioso.

Y alejóse de ellos para ir a una cantina a refrescar el gaznate.

—¿Por qué me dijiste que al tío le gustaba todo lo escocés? — preguntó Wally a su primo—. ¡Si lo único escocés que le gusta es el whisky!

—¡No sé!... ¿Y de qué le vendrá su entusiasmo a volar?

—Esa afición le debe venir de algún antepasado águila o avestruz.

—¿Águila? A mí me parece que avestruz...

Pasearon por el campo de aviación. Cerca de allí se había levantado un circo...

Una hermosa muchacha, llamada Grisette, era la bailarina y la principal atracción del espectáculo.

4

Los dos amigos al verla corrieron tras ella y se pusieron a su lado piropeándola graciosamente.

—¡No tengas miedo, niña, que aunque me veas vestido de corto, soy mayor de edad! — dijo Wally que era un muchacho de gran robustez.

Y acompañó sus palabras poniendo sus atrevidas manos sobre el lindo talle de la joven.

Esta le rechazó indignada, y volviéndole la espalda con desdén, dijo a Ray que era un muchacho de baja estatura:

—¡No me gusta su amigo! ¡Es muy grosero! ¡Sus galanterías son insultos!

—¡No le haga usted caso! ¡Es el escándalo de nuestra familia! — dijo Ray, dando un pellizco a su primo—. En cambio yo soy el orgullo de cuantos me conocen...

Grisette simpatizó en seguida con Ray... mientras Wally comprendía que por aquella vez su primito llevaba ventaja.

Grisette se abanicó y Ray le dijo si quería dejarle ver el abanico.

—¡Quédeselo como recuerdo mío!...

—Muchas gracias, señorita... señorita...

—Grisette...

—¡Precioso nombre! ¡No me olvidaré de él, ni de su propietaria!

Uno de los empleados del circo llamó a la

muchacha y ésta despidióse de su nuevo amigo y de Wally con el que no había congeniado.

Los dos primos siguieron paseando por el campo de aviación y varias veces sufrieron grandes sustos al ver avanzar aeroplanos que parecían lanzarse contra ellos.

Pasearon por el campo de aviación...

Un avión iba a aterrizar hacia el sitio donde los dos jóvenes se hallaban. El piloto les hizo señas para que se apartasen, pero ellos en vez de atenderlas, prosiguieron su marcha por el mismo sitio.

El aparato se desvió a un lado a fin de no atropellarles y lanzóse, entonces, contra un grupo de oficiales a los que causó varias contusiones.

El piloto se deshizo en excusas culpando de lo sucedido a los dos paisanos y corriendo hacia ellos con ánimo de exigirles responsabilidad.

Pero, los dos primos, comprendiendo que las cosas iban por lo serio, escaparon a toda velocidad y se escondieron en uno de los pabellones, donde se reparaban y construían hélices.

Las hélices volteaban vertiginosamente produciendo espantosas corrientes de aire.

Los dos primos se vieron envueltos en aquel torbellino desencadenado de viento que en pocos momentos se les llevó los vestidos dejándoles en ropa interior.

Los mecánicos que se hallaban fuera de la órbita del peligro, pararon instantáneamente los motores al ver aquel espectáculo, y los dos americanos, con erizada piel de gallina, abandonaron a toda prisa el taller. ¡Aquello era un ciclón!

—Bueno, ¿y qué hacemos ahora? — dijo Wally—. Porque con esa ropita, cualquiera va por el mundo.

—Lo que van a creer los franceses al ver-nos con esta indumentaria es que hemos venido de América para tomar parte en los Juegos Olímpicos.

—Busquémonos un traje en seguida... porque si nos descubren... nos hemos caído.

—¡Me huele la cabeza a pólvora!

Por fortuna descubrieron sobre el césped unos trajes abandonados de mecánicos y se los pusieron en el acto.

Pasó junto a ellos formado un grupo de mecánicos, y Wally y Ray, para no inspirar sospechas, se unieron al mismo.

Un oficial les pasó revista. Al hallarse ante Wally y Ray les preguntó señalándoles la espalda en la que faltaba lo que llevaban todos los demás:

—¿Dónde tienen ustedes los paracaídas?

—¡Oh! — contestó Wally, pálido y tembloroso—. ¡Nosotros no necesitamos!

—Es obligación usarlos para volar...

Les cargaron con aquella especie de mochila y un oficial les advirtió:

—¡No olviden las instrucciones! ¡En caso de necesidad tiren del anillo!

Iban a darse las inmediatas órdenes para efectuar un vuelo de reconocimiento.

Los dos primos se contemplaban con un susto de muerte en el corazón. ¿Qué iban a hacer? ¡Si les mareaban hasta los caballitos!

8

Y luego, si se descubría que no eran tales aviadores, iban a fusilarles.

—Hemos de escapar — dijo Wally a su pariente—. Esta gente me da más miedo que el ciclón.

Y procurando que nadie les viera corrieron a la desbandada por el campo hacia la salida.

Mas, un oficial descubrió su intento de fuga y con varios soldados siguió a los dos "desertores".

Viéndose alcanzados los dos americanos redoblaron los esfuerzos y Wally dijo:

—El oficial dijo que en caso de necesidad tirásemos del anillo. Me parece que tenemos que seguir las instrucciones.

Así lo hicieron, pero, al extenderse, el paracaídas les imposibilitó todavía más para correr y estuvieron a punto de ser cogidos.

Desciñéndose el cinturón lograron en el momento de peligro escapar y abandonar el aeródromo, internándose en los terrenos vecinos que ocupaba el circo Chelaine que había allí instalado sus tiendas...

Chelaine, el propietario del circo, decía en aquel momento a la concurrencia:

—¡Mi hija Grisette pasará la pandereta! ¡Vuestra generosidad será debidamente apreciada por todos los artistas!...

Wally y Ray llegaron al circo y se oculta-

ron entre el público. Al verles, Grisette avanzó hacia ellos y sonrió a Ray con gran afecto.

—¿Conque son ustedes aviadores?—les dijo.

—¡Si!... ¡Ya vé! ¡Alguna cosa hay que ser!
— dijo Ray.

—*¡Mi hija Grisette pasará la pandereta!*

—¿Les gustaría subir en nuestro globo cautivo?

—¡Oh... verá!...

No querían sentar plaza de cobardes ante
aquella muchacha... pero... eso de subir a las
alturas... como los angelitos...

Un hombre, el profesor Saenger, llamado el "rey del aire", que era el que tripulaba el globo cautivo en el circo, se acercó a Grisette y le dijo:

—¡No quiero que coquetees con los aviadores!

Los dos primos, siempre esquivando el peligro, se alejaron de nuevo...

El profesor Saenger era un espía que se dedicaba a transmitir información secreta al enemigo.

Wally y Ray recorrieron el circo y de pronto al apoyarse en un tablero se sintieron pinchados en la parte posterior de su cuerpo.

Wally creyó que su amigo se divertía con él y Ray pensó lo mismo.

—¿Quién te ha dado a ti derecho de propasarte? — le dijo.

—¡El que se está propasando eres tú!...

De nuevo sintieron un pinchazo. Indagaron. ¿Qué podía ser? Wally sacó la cabeza hacia la otra parte del tablero y vió a un hombre que lanzaba unos cuchillos contra una mujer apoyada en el madero.

Eran dos artistas del circo.

Un nuevo cuchillo vino a caer casi sobre la nariz de Wally, y éste, horrorizado ante la idea de perder algún órgano de su cara, se retiró seguidamente de allí.

De pronto, los dos primos vieron a unos oficiales de aviación que rondaban por allí cerca y temieron que les fuesen a detener.

Entraron en una tienda cambiando sus vestidos de mecánicos por unos uniformes exóticos que habían dejado allí unos artistas. De este modo, tal vez no les conociesen...

El globo que tripulaba el espía estaba ya en lo alto.

Wally y Ray protegidos por sus trajes no fueron reconocidos por los oficiales aviadores. Estos no tenían el propósito de detener a los dos americanos, sino de descubrir otra cosa más seria e importante.

—Desde que llegó el circo, los ataques aéreos del enemigo son mucho más frecuentes y eficaces — dijo un oficial al señor Chelaine—. ¡Creo que en el circo hay un espía que da información secreta al enemigo! Tal vez en el globo...

Al escuchar aquellas palabras a nadie cupo duda de que Saenger, cuya conducta había parecido sospechosa de un tiempo a aquella parte, era el espía peligroso.

Los dos americanos que eran grandes patriotas, quisieron hacer una de las suyas y agarrando un hacha se dispusieron a cortar la cuerda en que estaba sujeto el globo.

El espía Saenger, viendo el peligro aterrizó inmediatamente y saltando de la barquilla, metió en ella a los dos primos, y cortando las cuerdas dejó por completo libre el esférico... Luego huyó...

Wally se hallaba tan distraido que no se dió cuenta de que volaban hacia las nubes. Y al descubrir, por fin, que el globo iba a la deriva le entró, lo mismo que a su compañero, un pánico espantoso...

Los dos comenzaron a disputar, dándose cada uno la culpa de su mala suerte.

—¡Si dentro de dos minutos no me has dicho adónde vamos, te echo de aquí aunque seas mi primo! — gritó Ray.

—Cuando pase una golondrina se lo preguntaré — respondió Wally.

—¡Socorro!... ¡Socorro! ¡Qué desgracia la nuestra, haber venido a parar aquí!

Y el globo seguía subiendo.

—¿Qué vamos a hacer? Nuestra situación es realmente desesperada...

—Me dijeron una vez que echando lastre los globos descienden.

Y tiraron al aire varios sacos de arena pero no consiguieron otra cosa que aligerar el globo y por lo tanto hacerlo subir más.

Veían muy cercana la muerte pues la velocidad del globo iba cada vez en aumento.

Ray encontró en la barquilla unos mapas y se los guardó en el bolsillo. ¡Tal vez podrían tener utilidad!...

*
**

El esférico en su vuelo había dejado ya atrás las líneas amigas, atravesando tierras ocupadas por el enemigo...

Pasaron horas, muchas horas...

Desde el globo, los dos tripulantes por fuerza distinguieron a numerosos soldados cuyos cascos de acero brillaban al sol.

—Alégrate, que "aterrorizamos" en territorio francés — dijo Wally.

—¡Estos no son franceses! ¡Son de los otros! — gritó Ray.

—¡Ya no nos queda más lastre! — dijo Wally al echar abajo el último saco de arena.

—Pues ya no nos queda más que un remedio para aterrizar de una vez. ¡Echar de aquí al más *pesado!*

—¡Conformes!

—Pues salta tú, que eres el más *pesado...*

—¡No, señor, tú lo eres más!

Disputaron y llegaron a las manos... Wally accedió como un hombre de más peso a saltar del globo. Colocóse un paracaídas que halló en el globo y se lanzó al espacio.

Mientras tanto los alemanes comenzaron a bombardear el globo, y Ray, viendo que la cabina estaba ya incendiada y que la situación se hacía insostenible, lanzóse también al aire extendiendo otro paracaídas...

Momentos después ambos primos se encontraban en tierra junto a las márgenes de un río.

Se hallaban en territorio alsaciano. Si los alemanes les cogían... podían ya despedirse de sus cabezas.

Procurando ocultarse de la vista de unos soldados que por allí paseaban, encontraron abandonada entre unos arbustos una vaca de cartón tan estupendamente simulada que de lejos daba el engaño al más lince. Dentro de la vaca podían cabalgar tranquilamente dos hombres simulando las cuatro patas del animal.

Estaban salvados.

—¡Nos esconderemos dentro! — dijo Ray—. ¡Yo seré la cabeza de la vaca y tú la cola!

—¡Prefiero ser cabeza de vaca que cola de ratón!

Porfiaron y finalmente Wally ocupó la cabecera de la mesa ...¡ay!... de la vaca... y Ray se aposentó en la parte trasera.

Y de esta manera comenzaron a caminar en busca de una problemática libertad.

Cerca de allí se levantaba una modesta casita.

Durante las varias horas que navegaron en el aire se habían alejado tanto de París que se hallaban en la tierra de Alsacia...

La cercana casa estaba convertida en cuartel general de una brigada alemana.

Era la casa de la madre de Grisette, la bailarina del circo, una mujer alemana de nacimiento y que, naturalmente, hacía cuanto podía por servir a sus compatriotas.

Metidos en la vaca los dos americanos rondaban por los alrededores de aquella casita.

Al ver a un grupo de soldados, Wally dijo a su primo:

—Cuando pasemos por delante de ellos haremos el paso alemán y se creerán que somos una vaca de su país...

Y así lo hicieron... y los alemanes se tragaron el anzuelo.

En la casa, un oficial alemán dijo a un soldado:

—¡Vaya a ver si encuentra una vaca y tráigame un vaso de leche fresca!

El soldado salió con un bote y al ver a la vaca "Wally y Ray" quiso cogerla, pero la vaquita comenzó a saltar, y le costó enormes sudores conseguir detenerla.

La llevó a un establo y la dió de comer

paja. La "vaca" rechazó aquel alimento.

Dentro de ella, Wally dijo a su primo:

—¡El tío ese se empeña en que comamos paja!...

—¡Anda, cómela tú, que haces de cabeza!... — dijo Ray.

—¡Atiza! ¡Ahora quiere ordeñarnos!

—¡Esto es más difícil que comer paja!

—¡Espabílate, canastos! ¡Hemos de salir del mal paso!

El alemán se sentó en el suelo y buscó las ubres... de la vaca. Ray, repentinamente inspirado sacó por un agujero de la vaca sus manos que el soldado comenzó a estrujar... para sacar la leche, creyendo que eran las ubres.

Wally gritó:

—¡Cómo aprieta ese hombre, diablo!

Habló en voz tan recia que el soldado alemán le oyó y escapó, horrorizado de que las bestias hablasen.

—¡Señor, señor! — dijo al oficial—. ¡La vaca habla inglés!

Le rechazaron de allí creyendo que le había dado un repentino ataque de locura.

La vaca salió del corral y al avanzar por el camino cayó al suelo, rompiéndose en dos pedazos.

Partida de este modo siguió andando, pero

los soldados alemanes corrieron hacia ella y la detuvieron...

¡Ah! Conque dos hombres, ¿eh? ¡Dos espías, de seguro! Darían los fusiles buena cuenta de ellos.

Les condujeron a la casa de Grisette, presentándolos ante el comandante.

Wally y Ray se vieron perdidos.

—¡Nos han fastidiado! — dijo Ray, en voz baja—. ¡Hay que inventar un medio! Verás, les diremos que somos de los suyos...

—Tú los entiendes, pero, ¿cómo me arreglaré yo para que no me fusilen? — dijo Wally.

—¡Finge que eres sordo y mudo de nacimiento y contéstales con signos!

Ray no tenía nada de tonto. Recordó en aquel instante que en el globo había encontrado unos mapas, que se dejó indudablemente el verdadero espía Ray; y como los había guardado por si podían servirle para algo... ahora le vendrían de perilla.

Sin decir nada entregó los mapas.

El comandánte los examinó y luego dijo, trocando su ferocidad en una sonrisa:

—¡Estos son los mapas que nos hacían falta! ¡Magnífico! ¡Es un orgullo para mí tener bajo mis órdenes un par de excelentes espías como ustedes!...

18

—¡El orgullo es nuestro! — contestó Ray.

—¿Qué preguntan? — dijo Wally, por medio de signos.

—Nos preguntan si nos aburríamos dentro de la vaca.

—¡Vamos a dar un banquete en honor de ustedes por su heroico comportamiento! — dijo el comandante.

Poco después se daba una espléndida comida en honor de los dos americanos a quienes se les acababa de entregar unos uniformes militares.

Después de la comida, Wally y Ray vieron a una hermosa muchacha que paseaba por el salón. Era exactamente igual, idéntica, a la Grisette vista en el circo de París.

Los dos americanos se dirigieron hacia ella. Ray la pretendió abrazar, pero la joven le rechazó a lo lejos. ¿Quién era aquel hombre tan antipático... y de tan corta estatura? — pensó. En cambio, le gustó Wally por su buen tipo y atlética figura...

Ray, extrañado por aquel cambio, pues Grisette le prefería siempre a él y no a su compañero, le mostró el abanico que ella le había dado antes y dijo:

—¿Es que ya no te acuerdas de mí, Grisette, de cuando estabas en el circo de París?

—¡Oh, cómo se confunden ustedes! — dijo

la mocita—. ¡Yo soy Griselle y usted debe referirse a mi hermana Grisette! ¡Somos gemelas! ¡Ella fué a Francia con papá y es muy francófila!

—Son ustedes como dos gotas de agua...

—¡A mí me gusta más usted! — dijo Wally.

Grisette sonrió y sólo tuvo palabras cariñosas para este hombre. La ley de las compensaciones se cumplía allí una vez más. Ray era el preferido de la otra hermana.

✱✱

Algo más tarde, entró un jefe militar y dijo:

—¡Los americanos han ocupado este sector! ¡Necesito dos buenos espías para averiguar la posición exacta!

Un oficial propuso entonces a los soldados:

—¡Necesitamos dos voluntarios para un trabajo de espionaje en las líneas enemigas!

Wally murmuró al oído de su compañero:

—¡Ahora es cuando nos escabulliremos de aquí! ¡Ofrezcámonos!

Y avanzando hacia el jefe le dijo:

—¡Sería un placer muy grande para nosotros el poder meternos en las líneas enemigas!

—¡La patria se lo agradecerá! ¡Vengan conmigo!

Fueron a un cercano campo de aviación. Un aeroplano pintado de negro con una calavera y tibias en uno de sus lados, parecía esperarles.

El jefe les dijo:

—Si encuentran a los americanos desprevenidos, salten del aeroplano con el paracaidas y esta será la señal de ataque.

Wally dijo en voz baja a Ray:

—Una vez estemos entre los nuestros, que nos echen galgos.

—¿Qué ha dicho el mudo?

Wally fingiendo repentinamente mudez hizo con las manos unos cuantos signos arbitrarios.

El jefe llamó a su ayudante y le dijo:

—¡Fritz, usted que entiende el lenguaje de los mudos, pregúntele qué dijo!

Fritz efectuó diferentes movimientos con las manos que contestó con igual procedimiento, aunque sin entender palabra, el desdichado Wally.

Fritz no confesaba su ignorancia por aquel lenguaje que a él le era desconocido. Y dijo a su superior:

—¡Dice que siente mucho no tener siete vidas como los gatos para darlas todas por la patria!

En aquel instante apareció el aviador que

debía conducir el aeroplano. Era Saenger, el que subió al globo cautivo, un espía de cuidado que acababa de llegar a las líneas germanas, huyendo de la persecución enemiga.

Reconoció a los dos hombres que debían acompañarle. ¡Ah, los pillos del circo de París!...

¡Qué deseos tenía de vengarse de ellos! Pero, no quiso confesar lo que había ocurrido, anhelando castigar a aquellos audaces sujetos por su propia mano justiciera.

—¿Estos son los héroes que he de llevarme? — dijo.

—¡Los mismos! ¡Dos espías de primera clase! — contestó el jefe.

—¡Los conozco a los dos!... ¡No sé por qué me parece que éste será el último vuelo que hacen por la patria!...

Wally y Ray reconocieron a su vez al antipático individuo del circo y temieron por sus cabezas. Pero, ya que no decía nada, ellos optaron igualmente por callar...

Subieron al avión después de serles dadas por el jefe las últimas instrucciones.

El aeroplano emprendió rápido y majestuoso vuelo...

Los tres hombres guardaban un silencio hostil que parecía encerrar terribles ideas de muerte.

Saenger, que era patriota ante todo, pensó vengarse de sus enemigos más tarde, al regresar, una vez hubiesen cumplido su misión. Y por el momento fingió no acordarse del pasado.

Y después de afrontar miles de peligros reales e imaginarios, nuestros dos héroes aterrizaron en las líneas americanas...

Pero al hacerlo unos soldados yanquis les detuvieron. El avión se vió rodeado de enemigos; pero abriéndose paso, Saenger pudo de nuevo ganar los aires.

Wally y Ray quedaron prisioneros y fueron llevados inmediatamente ante la casa que servía de cuartel general...

Un sargento comunicó a su teniente lo sucedido.

—¡Un aeroplano enemigo acaba de aterrizar en nuestras líneas! Dos hombres desembarcaron de él e intentaron escapar, pero los hemos capturado. ¡Son dos espías!

—¡Tráigame a esos espías! — dijo el oficial.

— ¡Los ejecutaremos inmediatamente!

Al ver a Wally y Ray, el teniente se sorprendió. Conocía a estos dos hombres. Eran aquellos que habían movido tanto alboroto en el aeródromo y en el taller de reparaciones.

—¿Conque estáis aquí de vuelta? — les dijo—. ¿Qué mal aire os ha traído?

—¡Fuimos a dar un paseíto porque aquí nos aburríamos! — dijo Ray.

—¡Yo les mandaré a los dos a un lugar donde no se aburrirán!

En vano Wally y Ray intentaron defenderse. El oficial dió orden de que fuesen fusilados.

Iban ya a salir de la estancia, cuando entró un capitán.

—¡Dos espías... mi capitán!... ¡Los ejecutaremos en el acto!

—¡Se ha excedido en sus funciones, teniente! ¡Yo veré qué hago con ellos! — replicó el superior con acritud.

Los dos presos vieron el cielo abierto.

—¡Voy a buscarle una silla, mi capitán! — dijo Ray—. ¡Estos asuntos hay que tomarlos con calma!

Le acercó una silla; el capitán fué a sentarse, pero, distraído, Ray la apartó a un lado y el militar vino a caer en tierra causándose un fenomenal chichón en la cabeza.

—¡Fusile a estos dos espías al romper el alba, llueva o haga sol! — gritó el capitán, loco de ira.

Apareció entonces el comandante.

—¿Qué es eso? — preguntó.

—¡Dos espías, mi comandante! ¡Mañana los fusilaremos!...

—¡Se ha excedido en sus funciones, capitán! ¡Yo veré qué hago con ellos!

—¡Le daré una silla para que se siente!—dijo Ray.

Y otra vez acercó la silla y otra vez efec-

—¡Yo les mandaré a un lugar donde no se aburrirán!

tuó el juego de retirarla involuntariamente en el momento en que el comandante iba a tomar asiento.

El jefe dióse un golpe fenomenal en... salva sea la parte.

Levantándose, gritó:

—¡Fusilen inmediatamente a este par de esperpentos!

Los dos primos creyeron que aparecería un coronel para juzgarles, pero esta vez fué el fallo del comandante el definitivo.

Rodeados de un piquete salieron hacia el campo.

Les obligaron a ponerse junto a un muro...

Iban a mandarles al otro barrio con unas cuantas balas en el cuerpo.

Wally y Ray no perdían la serenidad ante la muerte.

Viendo a pocos metros de distancia a los soldados que se preparaban a apuntarles, Ray dijo:

—¡Si les estorbamos... avisen, que nos iremos!

El comandante dió orden para que todo terminara. Ocho fusiles se dirigieron hacia ellos apuntando su corazón...

Wally conservaba aún la serenidad, pero Ray en el momento definitivo, tembló pensando que aquella vez iban las cosas de veras.

Un oficial levantó el brazo. Iba a ordenar la descarga cerrada.

Como llovidos del cielo aparecieron en aquel

instante Grisette, la bella bailarina del circo
y su padre el señor Chelaine.

Wally dió un grito al ver a la muchacha y
tocó fuertemente a su amigo para que se fijara
en quién estaba allí.

*Wally y Ray no perdían la serenidad ante
la muerte.*

Ray, confundiendo el brazo de su primo con
una bala, cayó en tierra diciendo con voz do-
lorosa:

—¡Me han tocado! ¡Tráiganme un notario!

—¡No es eso, Ray! ¡Aquí tienes a Grisette!

—¡Grisette!

Acarició las manos de su amada, loco de contento, sin pensar que ante él tenía las ocho bocas amenazadoras de los fusiles.

El comandante y un oficial avanzaron hacia ellos.

Grisette lloraba negándose a moverse del muro. ¡Si tenían que morir... moriría también ella!

—¡Estos hombres no son espías! — dijo Grisette a los militares—. ¡El espía es aquel otro hombre! ¡El aeroplano en que iba sufrió una avería y tuvo que aterrizar.

Señaló a un aviador alemán que estaba allí cerca y que a una orden del oficial americano avanzó junto al muro.

Wally y Ray reconocieron a Saenger.

—¡Este hombre es un espía! — decía Chelaine—. ¡Lo tenía en mi circo y en el globo tomaba notas en servicio del adversario! Por fin he podido cogerle en el momento en que él aterrizaba.

Saenger negó la veracidad de aquellas palabras.

—¡Yo no soy más que el piloto del aeroplano! — dijo—. ¡Los espías son ellos dos!

—¡Pues todos fusilados! — gritó el comandante.

Dió orden para que los tres espías recibieran el regalito de las balas, pero Chelaine y su hija Grisette se negaban a marchar de allí, comprendiendo la inocencia de los dos americanos.

Apareció un automóvil y descendió de él un general.

—¿Qué ocurre? ¿Por qué se va a ejecutar a esos hombres? — dijo.

—¡Estos hombres no son espías!

—¡Son espías, mi general!... ¡Hace dos horas que trato de fusilarlos y no puedo!

—¡Se ha excedido en sus funciones, comandante! ¡Yo veré qué hago con ellos!

Avanzó hacia los americanos, quienes le contaron toda la verdad de la odisea.

—El piloto nos trajo aquí por la fuerza para que espiásemos la posición de las líneas americanas. Pero nosotros somos tan americanos como ustedes y sólo la mala estrella nos ha traído a tales andanzas — dijo Ray.

—¿Y qué tenían que hacer?

—Si las líneas están torcidas tenemos que dejarnos caer del aeroplano con el paracaídas para enderezarlas — dijo Wally—. ¡Estas son las órdenes!

—Pues ahora cumplirán las que yo les dé. Son ustedes demasiado listos para que se les fusile... Estamos preparados para resistir cualquier ataque. Subirán ustedes en el aeroplano y se dejarán caer en el paracaídas como les ordenaron. Los alemanes se engañarán... y nosotros podremos vencerles.

—¡Oh, no! — dijo Wally—. ¡No queremos volver en avión!

—Si no se dejan caer como les ordenaron, nuestros aeroplanos les harán a ustedes trizas...

El piloto alemán se negó a subir, pero bajo

el imperio de los revóveres, tuvo que acceder.

El avión conduciendo a Saenger y a los dos primos surcó los aires.

Otros aviones americanos les vigilaban.

Era preciso saltar... pero ninguno de los dos primos se veía con alma para efectuarlo...

—¡Si uno de los dos no salta, son capaces de hacernos saltar a tiros! — dijo Ray.

Prepararon los paracaídas... Saltando engañaban a los alemanes... Pero, en el momento de hacerlo, el piloto germano les encañonó un revólver, y les dijo:

—¡Prefiero que nos maten a ser causante de que mis compatriotas caigan en la trampa que les preparan ustedes!...

—¡Nada... nada... hay que saltar!

—¡Tiren los paracaídas y después salten si quieren! — gritó el alemán.

Los tres hombres se enzarzaron en violenta lucha...

En vista de que Wally y Ray no saltaban, desde un avión americano comenzaron a disparar contra ellos, causando grandes daños al aeroplano alemán que finalmente vino a tierra completamente incendiado, resultando muerto el piloto.

Por fortuna habían saltado antes los dos americanos provistos de los paracaídas y al bajar les esperaba una extraordinaria sorpresa: acababa de firmarse el armisticio...

Corrieron hacia el general, quien les dijo que no era ya necesario hacer nada, pues estaba concertada la cesación de hostilidades...

Y aclarado totalmente aquel asunto los dos americanos fueron puestos en libertad...

Y tras la terrible tempestad llegó la calma...

**

Meses después, habiéndoles su tio concedido permiso, Ray se casó con Grisette, la alsaciana francófila, y Wally, con Griselle, la germanófila.

El mismo barco les condujo a los Estados **Unidos.**

Las dos mujeres eran idénticas, tan iguales que se hubieran confundido si no era porque Grisette llevaba un perrito con un quepis francés y Griselle otro perrito con un saco alemán.

Aquellos distintivos servían para que los dos primos no confundiesen a sus mujeres.

—Nuestras respectivas mujeres son hermanas gemelas — decía Ray—. ¡De consiguiente somos cuñados gemelos!...

—¡Si primo era malo, cuñado es peor!... ¡No vayas a salir luego con que eres mi tía! — dijo Wally.

—¡Y suerte de los perritos que nos servirán para no equivocarnos de mujer!...

Y sin nuevos incidentes llegaron a su tierra para instalarse y vivir la existencia de la paz y del amor...

FIN

LA NOVELA PARAMOUNT

Publicación semanal de Argumentos de Películas
de la marca

Año II
N.º 62

PARAMOUNT

25
Cts.

EDICIONES BISTAGNE

PASAJE DE LA PAZ, 10 BIS — BARCELONA

RECLUTAS POR LOS AIRES

Chispeante comedia,

interpretada por los menos chispeantes

WALLACE BEERY y RAYMOND HATTON,
con una monada de criatura:
LOUISE BROOKS

Es un film PARAMOUNT

Distribuído por

PARAMOUNT FILMS, S. A.

"THE AIR RECRUITS"

A TRANSLATION OF "RECLUTAS POR LOS AIRES"

*This movie is dedicated to the brave aviators that fought
for freedom of the air for all kinds of birds except chickens.*

We are in the midst of the European war. In an aviation school on the outskirts of Paris, future "aces" were getting ready to confront every class of airborne enemy.

One morning three subjects with strange clothes including Scottish skirts came to the aviation field in an automobile.

They were Senor Angus and his two nephews, named Wally and Ray.

This Uncle was determined to become an aviator, in spite of having been rejected by two branches of the military, the army and navy, as being useless.

Wally and Ray had come from America to accompany their Uncle Angus on a great adventure.

But the air force rejected the longstanding candidate for being far too old, and Wally and Ray couldn't contain their laughter in seeing him fail.

"If you weren't my nephews and I had to pay for your burial, I would kill you both right now...."

And he walked away to a bar to wet his whistle.

"Why did you tell me that Uncle liked everything Scottish?" asked Wally to his cousin, "the only Scottish thing he likes is whiskey!"

"I don't know! Where does his enthusiasm for flying come from?"

"That affliction must come from some eagle or ostrich ancestor."

"Eagle? I'm thinking more ostrich."

They walked around the aviation field. Nearby, a circus tent had been raised.

A beautiful girl named Grisette was the show's dancer and main attraction.

The two friends ran towards her and started seducing her in an odd way.

"Don't be scared child, even if I'm dressed in a skirt I am a grown man!" said Wally, who was a very big man.

And he accompanied his words by putting his bold hands on her pretty body. Incensed, she rebuffed him, and turning her back, said to Ray, who was a short boy.

"I don't like your friend! He is very rude! His gallant words are an insult."

"Don't listen to him! He is the scandal of our family," Ray said pinching his cousin. "Rather, I am the pride of everyone that knows me."

Grisette immediately liked Ray… Wally understood why his cousin had an advantage.

Grisette was fanning herself, and Ray asked to see it.

"Keep it as a memory of me!"

"Thank you miss… miss…"

"Grisette."

"Beautiful name! I won't forget it, or its owner."

One of the circus employees called the girl and she said goodbye to her new friend and to Wally, who she didn't like.

The cousins kept walking around the aviation field and were scared many times by airplanes that seemed to be rushing towards them.

A plane was to land where they were standing. The pilot signaled them to move, but they kept walking around the site.

The airplane moved off to the side trying to avoid hitting them and crashed into a group of officials, causing many injuries.

They strolled through the aviation field…

The pilot tried to excuse himself by blaming the cousins, and ran towards them, saying they caused him to crash.

But the two cousins, sensing something was wrong, ran fast and hid in one of the shops where propellers were fixed.

The propellers were rotating just as fast, generating strong gusts.

The two cousins were caught in the whirlwind that took their clothes off, leaving them in their underwear.

Mechanics working in the shop saw the spectacle, and stopped the motors. Covered in goose bumps, the Americans hastily left the shop. That was a cyclone!

"Well, what do we do now?" asked Wally, "because with no clothes you can't just walk around."

"When the French see us in these clothes, they'll think we came to take part in the Olympic Games."

"Let's find suits, if they see us like this it's over."

"My head smells like gunpowder!"

Luckily they found abandoned suits lying on the grass and quickly got dressed.

A group walked past them, and not to raise suspicion, Wally and Ray joined the group.

An officer was making a routine check. Finding himself in front of Wally and Ray, he pointed to their backs, and asked why they were missing what everyone else had: "Where are your parachutes?"

"Oh!" Wally answered, pale and trembling. "We don't need those!"

"It is mandatory to use them during flight."

They put them on and the officer warned them: "Don't forget your instructions! In case of trouble, just pull the ring!"

Issues were ordered to make a reconnaissance flight.

The two cousins were starting to panic. What were they going to do? They got dizzy on a carousel!

But then, if someone discovered they weren't aviators, they would be shot.

"We must escape," said Wally to his relative. "These people are scarier than the cyclone."

And making sure no one saw them, they ran across the field.

But an officer, noting their escape, followed the two "deserters."

When they were trapped the two Americans doubled their efforts and Wally said: "The officer said to pull the ring in case of trouble, I think we should follow his instructions."

So they did, but the extended parachute made the run difficult and they were about to get caught.

Unfastening their parachute belts, they escaped in the nick of time and left the field, running to an area where the circus was putting up their tents.

Chelaine, the circus owner, told the audience: "My daughter Grisette will pass the tambourine around! Your generosity will be appreciated by our artists!"

Wally and Ray arrived at the circus and hid among the public. When Grisette saw them, she came closer and smiled at Ray with great affection.

"So you are aviators?" she asked.

"Yes! You see! You have to be something!" Ray answered.

"My daughter Grisette will pass the tambourine!"

"Would you like to go up in our air balloon?"

"Oh, you see…"

They didn't want to look like cowards in front of the girl… but going so high up… like angels.

Professor Saenger, who was called the "king of the air" because he manned the circus balloon, approached Grisette and said to her: "I don't want you flirting with the aviators!"

The cousins, avoiding danger, moved away again.…

Professor Saenger was a spy who transmitted secret information to the enemy.

Wally and Ray walked around the circus and soon; resting on a board, they both felt pinched on the backside.

Wally thought his friend was having fun with him, and Ray thought the same.

"Who gave you permission to touch me?" he asked.

"You are the one who touched me!"

What could it be? Wally looked around the board and saw a man throwing knives at a woman.

They were circus artists.

One knife came close to Wally's nose, and scared to lose any face organ, he moved away quickly.

Soon, the cousins saw aviation officials milling around, and feared arrest.

They entered a tent and swapped their mechanic's clothes for some exotic uniforms circus artists had left behind. In this way, they hoped they might not be recognized.

The balloon, manned by the spy, was in the air.

Wally and Ray, undercover in their new costumes, were not recognized by any one. The officers had not been assigned to arrest the two Americans, but to look into a more serious matter.

"I think there is a spy giving away classified information to the enemy! Maybe from the balloon… Since he came to the circus, enemy airstrikes have become much more accurate, and deadly" said an officer to Mr. Chelaine.

Now, there wasn't a shadow of doubt that Saenger, whose conduct was suspicious from the beginning, was the dangerous spy.

The two Americans, being big patriots, took an axe and attempted to cut the rope the balloon was attached to.

Saenger, sensing danger, quickly landed and jumped out, pushing the cousins inside and cutting its ropes and freeing the balloon.

Wally was so distracted that he didn't notice that they were rising up toward the clouds. Finding the balloon adrift, he and Ray began to panic.

The both started to argue, blaming each other for their bad luck.

"If you don't tell me where we are going in the next two minutes, I will kick you out, I don't care if you are my cousin," screamed Ray.

"When a swallow comes by I'll ask her," answered Wally.

"Help! Help! What a disgrace, how did we come to this?"

"What are we going to do? This is a real desperate situation."

"Someone once told me that throwing off weight makes the balloon come down." So they threw sandbags overboard, but that didn't make the balloon descend. They were going higher.

Death was near, as the hot air balloon ascended.

Ray found some maps in a box, they might come in handy!

The balloon had already moved past friendly ground and was now going over enemy territory.

Hours went by, many hours.

From the balloon, they made-out some soldiers whose helmets shined in the sun.

"Be glad we are landing in French territory," said Ray.

"Those are not French! They are the other guys!" screamed Ray.

"There is no more weight to lose!" said Wally, throwing out the last sandbag.

"Well, there is but one solution, to land at once. Out with the heaviest!

"All right!"

"Well you jump, you're heavier."

"No sir, you are!"

They argued and got into a fight… Wally, admitting he was heavier, decided to jump from the balloon. He put on a parachute and jumped into the air.

Meanwhile, seeing that the Germans had started to bombard the balloon, and it was starting to catch fire, Ray also jumped out with his parachute.

Moments later, both cousins were standing close to a river.

They were on Alsacian grounds. If they were caught… they could say goodbye to their heads.

While hiding from some soldiers that were passing by, they found an abandoned cardboard cow, so beautifully crafted, that it could fool anyone. Inside of it, two men could easily ride, simulating the four legs of the animal.

They were saved.

"We will hide inside!" said Ray. I'll be the head and you'll be the tail!

"I'd rather be a cow's head than a mouse's tail."

They struggled and finally Wally occupied the head of the table… Oh!… of the cow… and Ray settled for the rear.

They started walking, looking for freedom.

During the long hours in the air, they had flown so far from Paris that they were now in Alsacia.

There came across a little house, which served as headquarter of a German brigade.

It turned out to be Grisette's mother's house, the circus dancer, who was German by birth. Grisette's mother would do anything to serve her country.

Inside the cow, the two Americans were coming closer to the house.

Seeing a group of soldiers, Wally said to his cousin: "When we go by them, we will do the German march, so they think we are a German cow."

So they did… and the Germans took the bait.

Inside the house a German official said to a soldier: "Go see if you can find a cow and bring me a glass of fresh milk!"

The soldier went out with a bucket and tried to catch the "Wally and Ray" cow, but the little cow started jumping, and he went through great pains to stop it.

He took it to a stable and fed her hay. The "cow" rejected the food.

Wally said to his cousin: "This man wants us to eat hay!"

"OK, you eat it, you're the head!" said Ray.

"Damn! He is trying to milk us!"

"This is harder than eating hay!"

"Get it together! We will get out of this situation!"

The German sat on the ground and started looking for the udders… of the cow. Ray, suddenly inspired, put his hand and fingers out through a hole, and the soldier started squeezing.

Wally screamed: "Man this man can squeeze!"

He spoke in such a deep voice that the soldier ran off scared that beasts could talk.

"Sir, sir!" he said to the officer. "This cow speaks English!"

They blew him off, thinking he had some sudden attack of madness.

The cow came out of the corral and fell on the ground, splitting into two pieces. It continued on until German soldiers saw it and ran towards the cow and stopped it.

"Oh, two men? Two spies for sure! We should let our rifles decide."

They were taken to Grisette's house.

Wally and Ray thought they were about to die.

"We're screwed!" said Ray in a whisper. "We have to come up with some excuse! We'll tell them we're on their side."

"You can understand them? How will I manage not to get shot?" said Wally.

"Pretend to be a deaf-mute and answer in signs!"

Ray was no fool. He remembered he had found some maps that the real spy left. And he knew they would come in handy.

Without saying anything he handed them the maps.

The commander examined them, and turning his wrath into a smile and said: "These are the maps we were missing! Wonderful! It makes me proud to have such an excellent pair of spies working for us!"

"It is our pleasure!" answered Ray

"What are they saying?" Wally gestured.

"They asked if we were bored inside the cow."

"We will have a banquet in your honor of your heroic actions!" said the commander.

Later on, a great meal was served in honor of the two Americans. Each had been issued German military uniforms.

After eating, Wally and Ray saw a woman walking across the hall. She was identical to Grisette, the one in the Paris circus.

The two Americans approached her.

Ray tried to hug her, but the woman rejected him. "Who was this short man?" she asked. Instead she liked Wally for his athletic figure.

Ray, surprised by this sudden change in Grisette, showed her the fan she had given him before and asked:

"Do you not remember me Grisette, from the Paris circus?"

"Oh you are confused!" said the lady. "I am Griselle and you must have confused me with my sister Grisette! We are twins. She went to France with Father and is very Francophilic!"

"You are like two drops of water."

"I like you better!" said Wally.

Grisette smiled and said only kind things. The law of comparisons went into effect… Ray was the favorite of the other sister.

Later, a soldier came in and said: "The Americans have moved into this sector! I need two good spies to find out their exact position!"

Another soldier then announced: "We need two volunteers for a spy job behind enemy lines!"

Wally whispered into his partner's ear: "This is how we escape! Let's offer ourselves!"

Approaching the commander he said: "It will be our honor to sneak behind enemy lines!"

"Your country thanks you! Come with me!"

They went to a nearby aviation field. A black airplane with a skull and bones painted on it was waiting for them.

The commander said: "If you find the Americans are distracted, jump out of the plane using parachutes and that will be the sign for an attack."

Wally whispered to Ray: "Once we are with our forces, let them try and catch us!"

"What did the mute say?"

Wally, suddenly faking being a mute, made a few arbitrary signs.

The commander called on his assistant and said: "Fritz, you understand sign language, ask him what he said!"

Fritz made some hand gestures that Wally imitated without understanding a single thing.

Fritz did not understand anything as well, this language was unfamiliar. And he said to his superior: "He said he is sorry not to have seven lives like cats and to give them all for his country!"

A pilot appeared. It was Saenger, the one that was in the balloon, a sneaky spy who had just gotten behind German lines, fleeing enemy persecution.

He recognized the two men that were supposed to go with him. The two rogues of the Paris circus!

Saenger wanted revenge! But, he didn't want to confess what had happened because he wanted to take revenge with his own hands.

"These are the heroes that I must take with me?" he said.

"Yes! Two first class spies!" the commander answered.

"I know them both! I have a feeling this will be their last flight for the motherland!"

Wally and Ray also recognized the odd fellow from the circus, and feared for their heads. But, as he wasn't giving them away, they too opted to be quiet…

They got in the plane after being given final instructions.

The plane took a majestic fast flight.

There was such a hostile silence that the three men each felt that death was at hand.

Saenger, being a patriot first, decided to take revenge on his enemies after they got back, once they had fulfilled their mission. For the time being he pretended not to remember the past.

After confronting thousands of real and imaginary dangers, our heroes landed behind American lines.

When they landed they were caught by Yankee soldiers. The plane was surrounded, but Saenger managed to escape.

Wally and Ray were taken prisoner and brought immediately to a house that served as headquarter.

A sergeant informed his lieutenant what happened.

"An enemy airplane has just landed behind our lines! Two men tried to escape but we caught them. They are two spies!"

"Bring them to me!" said the officer. "We will shoot them immediately!"

When he saw Wally and Ray, the lieutenant was surprised. He knew these men. They were the ones that caused all that fuss in the mechanic's workshop.

"So you are back?" he said. "What misfortune brought you here?"

"We went for a stroll because we were bored!" said Ray.

"I will send you to a place you will never get bored!"

In vain, Wally and Ray tried to defend themselves. The officer gave the order to have them shot.

They were leaving when a Captain entered.

"Two spies... my Captain. We will execute them right away!"

"You are going too far Lieutenant! I will decide what to do with them!" replied his superior with a superior attitude.

Both prisoners saw their opportunity.

"Let me find you a chair Captain!" said Ray. Such decisions are to be made calmly!

He gave him the chair, but when the Captain was going to sit, Ray moved it and the military man fell to the ground and bumped his head.

"Shoot these two spies at dusk, come rain or sunshine!"screamed the Captain in rage.

Then a Major appeared.

"What is this?" he asked

"Two spies sir! We will shoot them tomorrow!"

"You are overstepping your authority! I will decide what to do with them."

"I will bring a chair for you to sit!" said Ray.

And once again he pushed it away just when he was going to sit.

"I will send you to a place you will never get bored!"

The Major came down hard on his private parts.

Getting up he screamed: "Shoot these pair of lowlifes immediately!"

Both cousins believed a Colonel would show up to judge them, but this time the ruling was final.

Surrounded by a pair of soldiers, they were taken out to a field.

They were put against a wall.

They were going to be sent to the other side with a few bullets holes.

Wally and Ray didn't lose their calm in the face of death.

Seeing the soldiers getting ready to aim at them, Ray said: "If we are in the way, just let us know and we will move!"

The Major gave the order to finish it. Eight rifles were aiming at their hearts…

Wally kept calm, but at the last moment Ray realized things were serious.

An officer raised his hand. He was ordering the soldiers to fire.

Like rain from the sky, the beautiful circus dancer Grisette suddenly came by with her father, Mr. Chelaine.

Wally screamed when he saw the girl and punched his cousin so he too noticed who was there.

Wally and Ray didn't lose their calm in the face of death.

93

Ray, confusing his cousin's arm with a bullet, fell to the ground saying in a painful voice:

"I've been hit! Bring a notary!"

"It's not that Ray! Grisette is here!"

"Grisette!"

He caressed her hands, happy as can be, without thinking he still had eight rifles pointing at him.

The Major and another officer approached them.

Grisette was crying, refusing to move away from the wall. If they had to die… she would die with them!

"These men are not spies! said Grisette to the soldiers. "The spy is that other man! The plane he was flying broke down and was forced to land.

She pointed at a German aviator that was close by, and was also put against the wall.

Wally and Ray recognized Saenger.

"This man is a spy!" said Chelaine. "He was in my circus and he took notes in his balloon for the enemy! At last, I caught him on the ground."

Saenger said it was a lie.

"I am only the plane's pilot!" he said. "Those are the spies!"

"Well, shoot them all!" screamed the Colonel.

He gave the order for the three spies to be shot, but Cherlaine and his daughter Grisette wouldn't move, believing the Americans innocent.

An automobile appeared and a General came out.

"What is going on? Why are you shooting these men?" he asked.

"They are spies General!... I've been trying to shoot them for the past two hours and can't."

"You are overstepping your authority, Colonel. I will see what to do with them!"

These men are not spies!

He approached the Americans, who told him the truth about the whole odyssey.

"The pilot brought us here against our will to spy on the American lines. But we are Americans like you, and only bad luck has caused us to do this."

"And what were you supposed to do?"

"If the lines were crooked, we were supposed to jump from the plane without our parachutes!" said Wally. "Those were the orders."

"Well now you will do what I say. You're too smart to be shot… We will be ready to resist any attack. Then you will go up in the plane and jump as you were told. The Germans will be fooled… and we shall defeat them."

"Oh no!" said Wally. "We don't want to get back in the plane!"

"If you don't jump as ordered, our planes will shoot you down…"

The German pilot refused to go in the plane, but under gunpoint, he was forced to.

The plane with Saenger and the two cousins flew into the air.

Other American planes were watching them.

It was necessary to jump, but neither of the cousins wanted to do it.

"If one of us doesn't jump, they will shoot us until we do!" said Ray.

They readied the parachutes… By jumping, they would trick the Germans… But at the last moment, the German pilot pulled a gun and said: "I would rather be killed than have my countrymen fall for your trap!"

"We have to jump! We have to!"

"Throw out the parachutes and then jump if you want!"said the German.

The three men got into a violent fight.

Seeing that they weren't jumping, a nearby plane started shooting at them, causing the German plane to come down in flames, with its pilot dead.

Luckily, the two Americans had jumped out just before the crash, and when they hit the ground there was a big surprise: the end of the war had been signaled.

They ran towards the General, who said it was no longer necessary to do anything, since a ceasefire was signed…

And so, with that matter cleared-up, the two Americans were set free.

And after the tempest, came the calm.

Months after, with his Uncle's approval, Ray married Grisette, the Francophile Alsatian and Wally married Griselle, who loved Germany.

The same boat carried them both to the United States.

The women were identical, so much so that they would have been confused if Grisette had not carried a French dog with a French cap and Griselle a German one with a German helmet.

That was the only way the cousins could keep from mixing them up.

"Our wives are twins" said Ray. "Therefore, we must be twin brothers in law!"

"As if cousins wasn't bad enough! Don't tell me you are my Aunt next!" said Wally.

"We are lucky to have the dogs to differentiate them!"

And without further incident they returned home to settle down and live a peaceful and loving existence.

THE END.

This page from a Spanish movie herald promotes
a showing of the film in November, 1928.

Louise Brooks, photographed by Eugene Robert Richee.

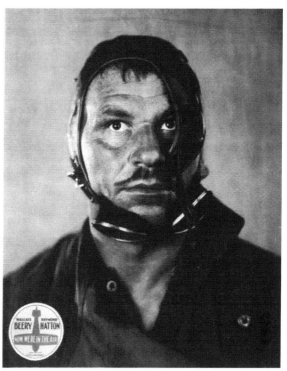

ČESKÝ SVĚT

Praha, 8. srpna 1929.   Číslo 46. Ročník XXV.

LOUISE BROOKS, představitelka Lulu ve filmu „Pandořina skříňka".

IN CZECHOSLOVAKIA

Louise Brooks, it might be said, was in vogue in Prague in 1929. To movie goers in the Czech capitol, the actress must have seemed everywhere.

Three of the actress' films, including *Now We're in the Air*, played in Prague that year, with two of the three proving popular enough to be shown on different occasions in different theaters. Brooksově (as she was sometimes called) was also celebrated in song, had her name in lights, and was the subject of articles in Czech newspapers and magazines. As she was in Berlin and Paris, Brooks was considered an important American star.

Now We're in the Air, under its Czech title *Rif a Raf, Piloti*, premiered in Prague at the Avion theater on June 21, 1929. The clipping reproduced below announces the film's opening, notes it would play a week, and that patrons would find it "neodolatelně," or "irresistible." In August, another of Brooks' 1927 films—*Rolled Stockings*, also played for a week at the Avion theater (under the title *Studenti z Calfoxu*), along with Chaplin's *A Woman of Paris* (1923). *Rolled Stockings* was the first film for which Brooks received star billing in the United States, and her name was duly noted next to the film title in the movie listings in Prague newspapers.

In November, *Rif a Raf, Piloti* returned to Prague for a second run, showing for a week at the Minuta theater, this time as part of a double bill alongside the prestigious 1928 Emil Janning's film, *Hříchy otců* (*Sins of the Fathers*).

Around the same time that *Rif a Raf, Piloti* was showing at the Minuta theater, it was also showing as part of a double bill (along with *Dvě čisté duše*) at the Nejstarsi bio Ponrepo on Karlova street, a theater

* * *
Od pátku dne 21, června 1929:
* **Kam se jit zasmát tento týden?** Jen do **Avionu** od zítřka na nejpovedenější frašku „Rif a Raf - piloti" ve kterém známí američti komikové **Walace Beery a Raymond Hatton** provádějí neodolatelné kousky.

7553

founded by the Czech magician and cinema pioneer Viktor Ponrepo. The theater billed itself as the oldest bio(graph) in the Czech capitol.

These second run showings of *Rif a Raf, Piloti* overlapped, as the 1929 newspaper advertisements shown here also indicates, on the same day that *Pandořina skřínka* (*Pandora's Box*) was playing in two Prague theaters, the Bio Na Slovanech and Bio Helios. In Czechoslovakia (as it was then called), the build-up around the new G.W. Pabst film was considerable. The 1929 German film starred Brooks as Lulu, and it also featured the debonair young Czech actor Franz Lederer (born František Lederer), as Lulu's lover. In what likely was an effort to promote both the film and Brooks role as Lulu, the actress' name appeared in lights in Prague as part of a widespread publicity push around the film. (see next page)

That publicity campaign included getting Brooks name in print, and talked about. In 1929, a number of articles about the actress and *Pandořina skřínka* appeared in the Czech press (including Czech film magazines); the actress also appeared on the cover of a leading Czech magazine, *Český svět*.

Brooks, as well, appeared on the sheet music for "Zasu," a song by the eminent Czech composer Jaroslav Ježek. "Zasu," a cabaret number, was performed in 1929 at the modernist Liberated Theatre, a theater described as the most popular and most relevant in Prague at the time. "Zasu" was also released as a 78 rpm recording.

To movie goers in Prague in 1929, Louise Brooks must have seemed everywhere, even, it might be said, *in the air.*

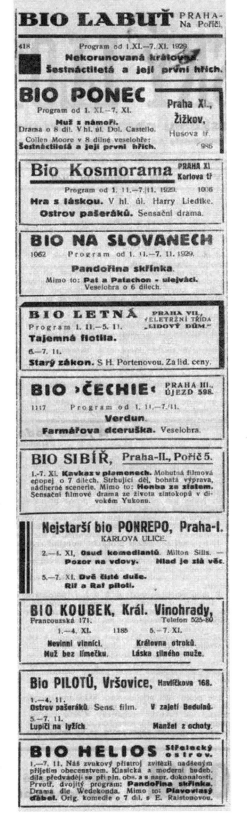

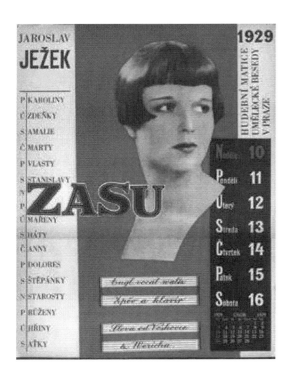

(Left) The sheet music for Jaroslav Ježek's cabaret hit "Zasu," which was performed at Prague's Liberated Theatre. The song was also recorded and released as a 78 rpm.

(Below) Brooks' name in lights above a Prague theater in 1929. The image comes from a 1930 Czech film annual surveying cinema highlights from the previous year.

This portrait, one of a series of Brooks in a black tutu, was issued as part of
the publicity campaign for *Now We're in the Air*.

LULU'S BLACK TUTU

Within Brooks' body of work, *Now We're in the Air* has received relatively little consideration. This negligence stems in part from its frivolous story as well as its decade's long status as a lost film. Naturally, what critics or film historians could not see, they would not give much thought.

After completing work on *Now We're in the Air*, Brooks was lent out to Fox for *A Girl in Every Port* (1928), a "buddy film" directed by Howard Hawks. For years, that film was thought to be the work which inspired German director G.W. Pabst to cast the actress as Lulu in *Pandora's Box* (1929). Seemingly, the first to make such a claim was George Eastman House film curator James Card in his 1956 article, "Out of *Pandora's Box*: Louise Brooks on G.W. Pabst." The claim was then repeated by others, including Brooks herself, in the years that followed.

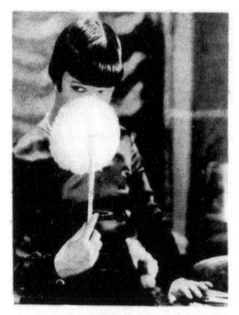

Kokett . . .
. . . oder verschämt?
Der Paramount-Star Louise Brooks

Pabst cast Brooks as Lulu approximately six months after the February, 1928 premiere of the Hawks' film—and after the conclusion of a well publicized, nationwide search for an actress in Germany. Not quite content with the resulting actresses (including by all accounts Marlene Dietrich), Pabst wrote to Paramount asking after Brooks. The German director was in search of a "different type."

Card's claim makes sense when considered as a sequence of events. Likewise, the assumption that Pabst saw his Lulu in Hawks' Marie also fits, in that Brooks plays a "dangerous female" in each film.

As exhibition records make clear, however, American films showed in Europe months and sometimes a year or more after their American premiere. *Blaue jungens, blonde Madchen* (the German title of the Hawk's film) was shown in Germany in December, 1928, well after filming on *Pandora's Box* had finished. The question arises, how could Pabst—an independent filmmaker not allied to either Fox or Paramount, have seen *A Girl in Every Port* prior to its release in Germany? One might also ask, if Pabst didn't see *A Girl in Every Port* before he cast Brooks, what was it that called his attention to Brooks. Might it have been a newspaper or magazine clipping, like the one depicted on the previous page in which Brooks is described as a coquette?

If Pabst saw any of Brooks' films, it might have been one of her 1927 films. Was it *Evening Clothes* (*Ein Frack Ein Claque Ein Madel*), in which Brooks' is without her trademark bangs and wears her hair in a way not dissimilar to her appearance in the gambling boat scenes near the end of *Pandora's Box*? Or was it *The City Gone Wild* (*Der Verbrecherkönig von Chicago*), in which Brooks plays the tough girlfriend of a gangster. Was it *Now We're in the Air* (*Riff und Raff als Luftschiffer*), in which Brooks dresses in a black tutu? Or might it have even been the 1926 film, *Just Another Blonde* (*Die Braut am*

Scheidewege), which showed in Berlin in March, 1928. Without a paper trail going back to 1928 or 1929, or a later statement by Pabst, we may never know for certain what caught the director's eye and inspired him to consider Brooks for the role of Lulu. Was James Card making an assumption when he declared it *A Girl in Every Port*?

A clue, of sorts, might be found in *Pandora's Box*. In the scene near the end of the film which takes place aboard a gambling boat, Lulu is pimped to a man wearing a fez. In order to entice the man to purchase Lulu's services, he is shown three pictures of Lulu in various outfits. Each outfit is meant to allure. One of the pictures is a widely distributed Paramount publicity photo of Brooks in the familiar black tutu, the same outfit the actress is seen wearing in *Now We're in the Air*.

Coincidence perhaps. Clue, perhaps as well.

This screen capture from *Pandora's Box* (1929) shows Louise Brooks in the
black tutu worn by the actress in *Now We're in the Air* (1927).

All's well that ends well: at the conclusion of the film, the two heroes are reunited with their new wives, but the men can only tell the twins apart by their dogs— one a German breed, the other a French breed!

FILM CREDITS & TRIVIA

Studio: Famous-Players Lasky
Producer: Adolph Zukor and Jesse L. Lasky
Associate Producer: B.P. Schulberg
Director: Frank R. Strayer
Assistant Directors: Ivan Thomas, and William Kaplan
Writing Credits: Monte Brice and Keene Thompson (story); John Goodrich and
      John McDermatt (screenplay, uncredited contributions); Thomas J. Geraghty
      (screenplay), George Marion (titles)
Cinematography: Harry Perry
Second Cameraman: Alfred "Buddy" Williams
Assistant Cameramen: Al Myers and A. La Shalle
Akeley Cameramen: E. Burton Steen and assistant; Cliff Blackstone and assistant
Technical advisor: Capt. Harold Campbell
Film editor: Carl Pierson
Ladies wardrobe: Frank Richardson

Cast: Wallace Beery as Wally; Raymond Hatton as Ray; Russell Simpson as Lord
      Abercrombie McTavish; Louise Brooks as Griselle & Grisette Chelaine; Emile
      Chautard as Monsieur Chelaine, father of the twins; Malcolm Waite as Professor
      Saenger; Duke Martin as Top Sargeant; Richard Alexander as German officer
      (uncredited); Theodore von Eltz as German officer (uncredited); Fred Kohler
      (uncredited); Charles Stevens as Knife Thrower (uncredited); Mattie Witting
      as Madame Chelaine, mother of the twins (uncredited).

Now We're in the Air was officially released October 22, 1927, with a stated length of 6 reels (5,798 feet), or approximately 60 minutes. [Pre-release Paramount production records list the film at 6 reels (5,811 feet) for the domestic release, and 6 reels (5,782 feet) for the foreign release.]

As was usual for the time, the film opened in the United States ahead of its release date; the first showings took place on October 17, 1927 in Atlanta, Georgia, El Paso,

Texas, Kansas City, Missouri, Nashville, Tennessee and elsewhere. Fuzzy Woodruff, writing in the *Atlanta Georgian*, was the first to review the film. He opined, "Nothing however can take away from the roaring technique of the two stars, nor can any subject dim the luster of the beauty of Louise Brooks."

In America's non-English language newspapers and magazines, *Now We're in the Air* was generally advertised under its American title. However, in the Spanish-language press of the time, including the New York City-based *Cine-Mundial*, as well as the Paramount Spanish-language house organ *Mensajero Paramount*, the film was promoted under the title *Reclutas por los Aires*. In Portuguese-language newspapers, the film was advertised under the title *Agora Estamos no Ar*.

As an important release from a major studio, the film was shown around the world. Under its American title, documented screenings of the film took place in Australia, British Malaysia (Singapore), Canada, China, India, Ireland, Jamaica, New Zealand (see 1928 advertisement this page), Union of South Africa, and the United Kingdom (England, Isle of Man, Northern Ireland, and Scotland). In South Africa's *Cape Times* newspaper, the film was deemed "The success of the week."

Elsewhere around the world, *Now We're in the Air* was shown under the title *Deux Braves Poltrons* (then French Algeria); *Dos tiburones en el aire* (Argentina); *Riff und Raff als Luftschiffer* (Austria); *Nous sommes dans les air* (Belgium); *Dois aguias no ar* (Brazil); *Reclutas por los Aires* (Chile); *Rif a Raf, Piloti* (Czechoslovakia) and *Riff a Raff strelci* (Slovakia); *To muntre Spioner* (Denmark); *Nüüd, meie oleme õhus* and *Riffi ja Raffi õiged nimed* (Estonia); *Deux Braves Poltrons* (France);

Riff und Raff als Luftschiffer (Germany); *O Riff kai o Raff aeroporoi* (Greece); *Megfogtam a kemét!* (Hungary); *Katu Njosnararnir* (Iceland); *Nou Vliegen We* (Dutch East Indies / Indonesia); *Aviatori per forza* and *Aviatori … per forza* and *Ed eccoci aviatori* (Italy); *Yagi and Kita in the Air* (Japan); *Reclutas por los aires* (Mexico); *Hoerawe vliegen* and *Hoera! We Vliegen* (Netherlands); *Luftens Spioner* (Norway); *Riff i Raff jako Lotnicy* (Poland); *Recrutas Aviadores* (Portugal); *Riff es Raffal a foszerepekben* (Romania); *Reclutas por los Aires* (Spain); *Hjältar i luften* (Sweden); *Deux Braves Poltrons* (Switzerland).

The film's director, **Frank R. Strayer** (1891-1964), was an accomplished director, producer, and writer, and early on, an occasional actor. He was active from the mid-1920s until the early 1950s. Strayer is credited with directing 86 films. The high point in his career came in the late 1920's, when his credits included important films from major studios—*Rough House Rosie* (1927) with Clara Bow, *Moran of the Marines* (1928), with Richard Dix, and *Partners in Crime* (1928), with Beery, Hatton, Mary Brian, and William Powell. With the coming of sound, Strayer's prestige began to slip, and he was often assigned lesser fair and sometimes worked for poverty row studios. His later credits include dramas such as *Manhattan Tower* (1932), with Mary Brian and James Hall, and horror films, including *The Monster Walks* (1932) and *The Vampire Bat* (1933), the latter with Fay Wray. In the 1940's, he helmed 14 movies in a series based on the Blondie and Dagwood comic strip.

Wallace Beery (1885–1949), who plays one of the bumbling cousins, appeared in some 250 movies during a 36-year career. The year after *Now We're in the Air*, Beery played opposite Louise Brooks in *Beggars of Life* (1928), a story set among hoboes. In 1915, Beery starred with then wife Gloria Swanson in *Sweedie Goes to College*. Beery's other silent films include *The Last of the Mohicans* (1920), *The Four Horsemen of the Apocalypse* (1921), *Robin Hood* (1922), *The Lost World* (1925), *Old Ironsides* (1926), and *Casey at the Bat* (1927). Beery achieved his greatest fame in the sound era, alternating between comedic and dramatic roles. Today, Beery is best known for his portrayal of Bill in *Min and Bill* (1930) opposite Marie Dressler, as well as for *The Big House* (1930), for which he was nominated for an Academy Award, and *The Champ* (1931), for which he won the Academy Award for Best Actor. Beery also starred in *Grand Hotel* (1932) and *Dinner at Eight* (1933), as Long John Silver in *Treasure Island* (1934), and as Pancho Villa in *Viva Villa!* (1934). Beery was the brother of actor Noah Beery Sr. (who appeared alongside Brooks in *Evening Clothes*), and uncle of actor Noah Beery, Jr.

Raymond Hatton (1887–1971), who plays the other bumbling cousin, appeared in almost 500 movies, including a series of comedies in the 1920s paired with Wallace

Beery which marked the highpoint of Hatton's early career. Though he enjoyed success in the silent era, Hatton's career skidded during the sound era and he usually played smaller supporting roles, including the tobacco-chewing Rusty Joslin in "The Three Mesquiteers" Western series (though not in the installment featuring Brooks). In the 1950s and 1960s, he appeared in such TV series as *Dick Tracy*, *Adventures of Superman*, and *Leave It to Beaver*, as well as Westerns like *The Cisco Kid*, *Maverick*, and *Have Gun-Will Travel*. His last film role was *In Cold Blood* (1967).

Griselle and Grisette's Father, Monsieur Chelaine, was played by **Émile Chautard** (1864–1934). Chautard was a French-American film director, actor, and screenwriter active primarily in the silent era. He directed 107 films between 1910 and 1924, and acted in 66 films between 1911 and 1934. Beginning as a stage actor at the Odéon-Théâtre de l'Europe, he rose to the head of film production at Éclair Films' Paris studio in 1913, and soon emigrated to the United States. Between 1914 and 1918, Chautard worked for the World Film Company based in Fort Lee, New Jersey. There, in the company of a stellar group of other French-speaking technicians (including Maurice Tourneur, Léonce Perret, George Archainbaud, Albert Capellani, and Lucien Andriot), he directed and taught an apprentice film cutter, Josef von Sternberg. In 1919, Chautard hired von Sternberg as his assistant director on the film *The Mystery of the Yellow Room*, which Chartaud wrote, directed and produced. Choosing Hollywood over a return to post-war France, Chautard went to work for American studios such as Famous Players-Lasky. He received a few high-profile assignments, including Colleen Moore and Billie Dove vehicles. Chautard stopped directing in 1924, though he continued to make film appearances including acting roles in *Bardelys the Magnificent* (1926), *Seventh Heaven* (1927), *Lilac Time* (1928), and von Sternberg's *Morocco* (1930) and *Shanghai Express* (1932). In the von Sternberg film *Blonde Venus* (1932), he appeared as "Night club owner Chautard." His last role, an uncredited part, was in the Wallace Beery vehicle *Viva Villa!* (1934).

Russell Simpson (1877–1959) played the eccentric Uncle, Lord Abercrombie McTavish. His character's original name was Angus McWheelbase.

Also appearing in small roles in both *The City Gone Wild* and *Now We're in the Air* was **Duke Martin** (1894–1956). He also had a role in *Moran of the Marines* (1928).

Tall **Malcolm Waite** (1892–1949), who plays Prof. Saenger, played a spy in the previous Beery-Hatton movie, *We're in the Navy Now* (1926). Waite played a heavy in *The Gold Rush* (1925), and had roles in *Kid Boots* (1926) and *Noah's Ark* (1928).

WALLACE BEERY TALKS ABOUT HIS NEW FILM

"Now We're in the Air" Coming Here Today.

In Hollywood, among other rare and strange flora and fauna, there are actors who live their roles.

Wallace Beery and Raymond Hatton are not among them.

Should an actor who has played a crook part take up the burglary trade after working hours to keep in character? Should an actress lightly discard her precious morals when she is called upon to enact a fallen jezebel?

"It would be tough for Hatton and me if we lived our roles," said Beery. "It is so important for us not to live our roles that we have to step in and out of character every time we go before the camera.

"When you play a boob on the screen think what would happen if you lived your role after working hours, as so many of our colleagues are popularly rumored to do.

"Within a week Ray and I would have put our life savings, meager as they are, into fake oil stocks, we would have been run down by every sort of mechanical conveyance from scooters to freight trains, we would have been lost twice daily trying to find our way back and forth from the studio, if we were going any place we would always catch the wrong train, we would always be stumbling over something and something would always be falling on us.

"It's all right for guys like Adolphe Menjou and Richard Dix to live their roles. They're always playing smart people. We're just a couple of boob aviators in 'Now We're in the Air,' which will be at the Regent today, and I don't want to live that role when I go flying or I won't live to act another role."

SYNTHETIC AIR FLYING LATEST!

Wallace Beery and Raymond Hatton Produce 'It' in Mission Comedy

"Synthetic aviation is the newest hobby of Wallace Beery and Raymond Hatton, Paramount comedy stars," says Manager Pettis of the Mission theatre.

"Synthetic flying is done in airplanes fastened to a steel tower around which they revolve. It is a popular form of amusement at the beach resorts around Hollywood where Beery and Hatton were introduced to it for a sequence of their new picture, 'Now We're in the Air,' which opens at the Mission today.

"One trip on these airplanes is generally enough for the stoutest souls," Mr. Pettis said.

Beery and Hatton, at the behest of their director, Frank Strayer, had to make half a dozen.

The picture, just recently released, is booked for a four day engagement at the Mission, inaugurating the theatre's new policy.

Under this policy vaudeville has been eliminated and the house will book only big time and high class pictures. A number of notable releases have been contracted for in coming weeks, Mr. Pettis said last night.

This advertisement for Truso perfume appeared in a Chicago, Illinois newspaper during the film's first run in the windy city in December, 1927. The film returned to Chicago, where it was shown in five theaters around town the following month.

Appearing in the film as German officers were the American-born actors **Richard Alexander** (1902–1989) and **Theodore von Eltz** (1893–1964). Alexander was a character actor with numerous roles to his credit, including small parts in *The Docks of New York* (1928) and *All Quiet on the Western Front* (1930). Just as prolific, Eltz appeared in *Bardelys the Magnificent* (1926) and other films.

Also appearing in an uncredited role is **Fred Kohler** (1887–1938), a "heavy" in numerous American films of the silent and early talkie eras. Prior to his bit in *Now We're in the Air*, Kohler had leading roles in Josef von Sternberg's *Underworld* and the James Cruze-directed *The City Gone Wild* (both 1927). In the latter, he played gangster Gunner Gallagher, whose girlfriend was Snuggles Joy, played by Brooks.

Publicity had it that **Charles Stevens** (1893–1964), a character actor who played the knife thrower, was the grandson of Geronimo. Stevens started in films as early as 1915, and had parts in a number of silent films starring Douglas Fairbanks. Stevens took on roles as a Native American, and appeared in numerous Westerns and action films including the Wallace Beery vehicle *Viva Villa!* (1934), *Geronimo* (1939), and *Border Bandits* (1946), with Raymond Hatton. Later, he transitioned to television, where he played Geronimo in two episodes of *The Adventures of Rin Tin Tin* (1954).

Mattie Witting (1863–1945), who reportedly played Griselle and Grisette's Mother, was an actress active from 1915 through the end of the silent era. Witting was married to actor A.E. Witting, and was often credited as Mrs. A.E. Witting. She appeared in the Lois Weber-directed *Shoes* (1916), and prior to *Now We're in the Air*, played screen mother to stars including Colleen Moore and Jackie Coogan.

Much was made at the time that *Now We're in the Air* was the first Beery or Hatton film in which the two comedians "got the girl." Noting that Beery and Hatton had long been numbered among Hollywood's unkissed male stars (along with Lon Chaney and Raymond Griffith), one article read "Romance has always been denied these two screen stars. In all their pictures they have struggled through reel after reel of hectic adventure in behalf of some dainty heroine only to see her lost to a handsomer and younger male rival, just about 50 feet ahead of the final close-up."

Long an East Coast actress, Louise Brooks first arrived in Hollywood on January 6, 1927. She was met at the train by her husband's friend, Monte Brice, who co-wrote the screenplay for *Now We're in the Air*.

FURTHER READING

As a popular American film from a major studio, *Now We're in the Air* was widely written about when first released. Articles, reviews, and other features appeared in just about all the major English-language newspapers, film magazines, and trade publications of the day including *Weekly Film Review*, Oct. 22, 1927; *National Board of Review Magazine*, Nov. 1927; *Canadian Moving Picture Digest*, Nov. 12, 1927; *Photoplay*, Dec. 1927; *Screenland*, Dec. 1927; *Detroit Saturday Night*, Dec. 3, 1927; *Variety*, Dec. 14, 1927; *Exhibitor's Herald*, Dec. 17, 1927; *Moving Picture World*, Dec. 17, 1927; *Film Daily*, Dec. 18, 1927; *Motion Picture News*, Dec. 23, 1927; *Billboard*, Dec. 24, 1927; *Harrison's Reports*, Dec. 24, 1927; *The Bioscope*, Jan. 26, 1928; *Kinematograph Weekly*, Jan. 26, 1928; *Parents*, Feb. 1928; *Film Spectator*, Feb. 4, 1928; *Motion Picture*, March 1928.

A comprehensive, annotated bibliography of related material may be found on the Louise Brooks Society website. What follows is a small selection of American articles and reviews from the time of the film's release, followed by a few contemporary citations.

"Royal – Now We're in the Air." *Kansas City Star*, October 16, 1927.
— "This film is said to have an increased love interest. It will at least have our interest since Louise Brooks is the heroine. We gather from the pictures we have seen of the production that Miss Brooks is some sort of circus performer, as she is shown succumbing to the temptation of abbreviated skirts. That is Miss Brooks's old weakness. But then it takes two to make such a costume shocking, one to wear it and one to look at it. The picture also includes Mr. Beery and Mr. Hatton in a number of goofy poses. Both seem to be in love with Miss Brooks. We hope Mr. Beery gets her, because Mr. Beery has, to our mind, the most fascinating kiss in the movies. He kisses as though all his previous life had been spent playing the saxaphone."

McNulty, John. "Absurd Aviation." *Columbus Citizen*, October 24, 1927.
— "Louise Brooks, a pretty thing, has little to do but walk around and show her legs, which are pretty and the only amusing things in the picture."

anonymous. "Fight Pictures Prove Feature At The Strand." *Portland Evening Express*, November 1, 1927.
— "Louise Brooks is the young lady who is the charming m'm'selle, and she does add something to the picture although [she is] unable to lift it entirely from the gutter type of comedy to which it sometimes descends."

anonymous. "New Films of Comedy, Romance and Melodrama on Photoplay Programs." *Philadelphia Public Ledger*, November 8, 1927.
— "In a helping way, Louise Brooks proves to be the real thing and it is to her that a lot of credit must go for her for her sincere work in a dual role."

anonymous. "Beery and Harry Again." *Washington Star*, November 13, 1927.
— "Louise Brooks as the leading lady, too, was a happy selection, it is said. Young, beautiful and charming, in this picture she is doubly so, because she's twins, or in other words she has a dual role. She is French and German as well as clever and cunning."

Feldkamp, Frances V. "Movie Reviews." *St. Louis Globe-Democrat*, November 14, 1927.
— "Louise Brooks is cast in a dual role of twin sisters, one sympathizing with Germany, the other siding with France in the conflict. She looks good in both parts."

Warren, George C. "St. Francis is Offering Beery, Hatton." *San Francisco Chronicle*, November 14, 1927.
— "… they are disporting themselves and making big audiences scream with laughter."

Soanes, Wood. "*Now We're in the Air* Opens at American." *Oakland Tribune*, November 21, 1927.
— "An effort was also made to inject a little romance into the manuscript by having Louise Brooks play twins so that both Beery and Hatton could get a wife without having to hire a pair of leading women."

Parsons, Louella O. "Now We're in the Air. Big Laughfest at Metropolitan." *Los Angeles Examiner*, November 25, 1927.
— "The memory of Wallace Beery's fine performances as a dramatic actor arises to taunt me every time I see him in a goofy role that calls for eccentric comedy…. The audience at the Metropolitan theater proved this by shrieking aloud at in actual glee over the Beery-Hatton combination …. Louise Brooks, in a dual role, looks very

young and very pretty even though she has very little to do. One would think playing a twin would keep her busy, but the whole film is Beery and Hatton."

Carey, Nick M. "Berry, Hatton Fly at Met." *Los Angeles Record*, November 25, 1927.
— "Miss Brooks has a dual role. She is pretty, as usual, but thinner, I would say. She hasn't a lot to do and does that very well."

McCormick, Ella H. "Reel Players." *Detroit Free Press*, December 5, 1926.
— "Does a picture require any more recommendation than for one to say that Wallace Beery and Raymond Hatton are its principals? There is yet to be a Hatton-Beery collaboration that doesn't keep its audience verging on the point of hysteria."

Tinee, Mae. "Wallace and Raymond Take a Little Flyer in Aviation." *Chicago Tribune*, December 6, 1927.
— "Louise Brooks as twins, is–are–a beautiful foil for the stars and if you think she doesn't marry both of them before the picture ends, why, cogitate again, my darlings."

anonymous. "The New Film." *The World*, December 12, 1927.
— "The plot from here on flops into such inextricable positions that incoherency is avoided only by the subtle subterfuge of aiming and sacrificing everything in an attempt to end it all with Beery in one set of girlish arms and Hatton in the other set of the same girl's arms. Louise Brooks is the welcome serious relief in an unwelcome comic background."

Cannon, Regina. "Louise Brooks Puts Snap in Now We're in the Air." *New York American*, December 12, 1927.
— "Miss Brooks is the brightest spot in *Now We're in the Air*, for she may be always depended upon to be interesting, trig and snappy."

Pelswick, Rose. "Diversified Fare for Film Fan at Capitol, Colony, Rialto." *New York Evening Journal*, December 12, 1927.
— "Louise Brooks, playing a dual role, makes a very decorative heroine."

H., J. K. "New Photoplays." *New York Post*, December 12, 1927.
— "Louise Brooks wanders in and out between gags. She is very beautiful. She is especially beautiful when seen beside Mr. Beery."

anonymous. "Comic Fliers in the Grand." *Pittsburgh Post-Gazette*, December 20, 1927.
— "Wallace Beery and Raymond Hatton are running Lillian Gish a close second in bucking the vicissitudes of life…. Louise Brooks is with them, in a dual role of a French and also a German sympathizer. Of course, Beery gets one girl and Hatton gets the other, but they never are sure just which they have, as the girls are twins."

anonymous. "On the Screen." *Rochester Democrat and Chronicle*, December 21, 1927.
— "*Now We're in the Air* is a logical successor to the other Beery-Hatton successes, *Behind the Front*, *We're in the Navy Now* and *Fireman, save My Child.* It shows the two popular comedians in the accidental role of aviators…."

L., J.M. "Beery-Hatton Team is Fair at Colonial." *Richmond Times-Dispatch*, January 3, 1928.
— "The team of comedians was fortunate this time in having Louise Brooks appear with them. Not satisfied, too, with having Miss Brooks appear as one heroine, they have her appear as twins, which does much to make the picture easy to enjoy."

"King Is Offering Big Laugh Show At 5th Avenue." *Seattle Times*, January 9, 1928.
— ". . . an absurd thing filled with laugh-provoking gags."

anonymous. "Beery, Hatton on Capitol Bill." *Sacramento Union*, January 25, 1928.
— "Comedy still reigns at the Capitol theater…. The qualities of the film are emphasized with the appearance of delectable Louise Brooks."

Black, Beatrice. "Motion Pictures for Children." *Parents*, February, 1928.
— "Sometimes vulgar, always senseless. But the children will like it and, although it is not the type of picture we would urge them to see, still it is too silly to be harmful, and unless your child is a nervous, excitable youngster, it won't hurt them."

M., C. "Beery and Hatton Funfest at Kaimuki." *Honolulu Star-Bulletin*, February 6, 1928.
— "There is not a bit of doubt that *Now We're in the Air* is one of the funniest comedies ever thrown on the screen in Honolulu."

Wolf, Howard. "Strand Has Standard Beery-Hatton Comedy." *Akron Beacon Journal*, May 2, 1928.
— "*Partners in Crime* seems to me no better than the much maligned *Now We're in the Air* and no worse than the universally praised *Behind the Front*."

Brooks, Louise. *Lulu in Hollywood*. New York: Alfred A. Knopf, 1982.
— includes autobiographical essays which touch on Brooks' film work

Paris, Barry. *Louise Brooks*. New York: Alfred A. Knopf, 1989.
— biography of the actress with passages on the film

Orriss, Bruce W. *When Hollywood Ruled the Skies: The Aviation Film Classics of World War I*. Hawthorne, CA: Aero Associates, 2013.
— includes a two page section on *Now We're in the Air*

Kririan, Shari. *San Francisco Silent Film Festival*. San Francisco, California: 2017.
— festival program, includes notes by Thomas Gladysz

Le Giornate del Cinema Muto. Pordenone, Italy: Giornate del Cinema Muto, 2017.
— festival catalogue, includes two page essay by Jay Weissberg

Louise Brooks poses with Keene Thompson, who co-wrote the screenplay for *Now We're in the Air*. In *Lulu in Hollywood*, Brooks described this as her favorite publicity still.

Robert Byrne presents Thomas Gladysz (right) with an analog gif player as
a thank you for assistance in the preservation of *Now We're in the Air*.

ABOUT THE AUTHOR

Thomas Gladysz is the Director of the Louise Brooks Society (www.pandorasbox.com), which he founded in 1995. He has authored numerous articles on early film, and contributed program notes to the San Francisco Silent Film Festival, University of Wisconsin Cinematheque, Brattle Theater, EbertFest, Syracuse CineFest, and Telluride Film Festival.

In 2010, Gladysz edited and wrote the introduction to the Louise Brooks edition of *The Diary of a Lost Girl*, the book that was the basis for the 1929 film. His audio commentary to *Diary of a Lost Girl* can be heard on the 2015 Kino Lorber release. In 2017, he authored *Beggars of Life: A Companion to the 1928 Film*, and provided an audio commentary to the Kino Lorber release. That same year, after assisting with the preservation of *Now We're in the Air*, Gladysz penned an article for the Huffington Post, "Long Missing Louise Brooks Film Found," and wrote the program notes to the film's San Francisco premiere.

Gladysz has mounted exhibits and lectured on Louise Brooks at the San Francisco Public Library, and has introduced her films at the Niles Essanay Silent Film Museum, Detroit Institute of Arts, and Action Cinema in Paris, France. He blogs regularly, and programs RadioLulu.

Robert Byrne, author of the introduction, is a film preservationist specializing in the restoration of early cinema and silent era motion pictures. Past restoration projects have included collaborations with: Library of Congress, EYE Filmmuseum, Cinémathèque française, Photoplay Productions, British Film Institute, Museum of Modern Art, Library of Congress, Gosfilmofond of Russia, Filmoteka Narodowa, and Národní filmový archiv. Restored titles include *Shoes* (1916), *The Spanish Dancer* (1923), *The Last Edition* (1925), *Phantom of the Opera* (1925), *The Half-Breed* (1916), *The Good Bad Man* (1916), *Sherlock Holmes* (1916), *Behind the Door* (1919), *Now We're in the Air* (1927), *The Birth of a Nation* (1915), *The Thief of Bagdad* (1924), and *The Three Musketeers* (1921).

Since 2004, Rob has served on the board of directors for the San Francisco Silent Film Festival where he currently serves as President.

Raymond Hatton, Louise Brooks and Wallace Beery
Courtesy of the Academy of Motion Picture Arts and Sciences

Printed in Poland
by Amazon Fulfillment
Poland Sp. z o.o., Wrocław